You CAN Go Home Again

You CAN
Go Home
Again

F. BURTON HOWARD

Bookcraft
Salt Lake City, Utah

Library of Congress Catalog Card Number: 92–85091
ISBN 0–88494– 861–7

First Printing, 1992

Printed in the United States of America

The Prodigal's Song

I would change my life, O Lord,
But how?
My feet are mired in pathways
Adopted long ago. And days are
Filled with empty tasks
That I must do.

Resolve is new but ebbs away.
Tomorrow?
Those selfsame tasks and walkways
Are sufficient unto it as well
And leave no time or place for what
The Spirit asks.

Now? O restless waves of conscience
Be still.
My heart is patched with promises.
The conflict rages on. The still
Small voice of "should" cries out—
But I resist.

Doubt. Resolve. Is there no rest?
And fear,
Unsure of what to do, or when.
Unsheltered from the fray, I
Long for peace but stumble on—bound
To yesterday.

What must I do, O Lord, must
Shadows
Of the past forever cloud the day?
What can I say or do, to let my song
Again be heard on that straight but
Shrouded way?

And so I cried, until at last
An answer
Came—clear, and familiar too.
It was not the first time I had
Heard the words, though they were
Strangely new.

"Begin again," the Spirit said,
"Ere day
Turns into day. As you once learned
To whistle, by wanting to,
Pursing childish lips till first faint
Music came,

"So now, though childhood virtues lie
Tarnished
And unused, Desire, which once
Brought all things within your grasp,
Will bring this too—and more—if you
But ask."

Could I but break the prison of all
I've done before,
And put off the former man,
No fear of welcome would ever slow
My anxious homebound
Step again.

It seemed I heard a voice which said,
"O ye
Who must needs change. How oft
I would have gathered thee. The door
Is open wide. The hour is late.
Come home."

I will. I will. Could there be place
For me?
There is. A place to grow and serve
And somehow be a part. To sing
A song of redeeming love. Be still,
My joyful heart.

"And he arose, and came to his father.
But when he was yet a great way off,
His father saw him, and had compassion,
And ran, and fell on his neck,
And kissed him." (Luke 15:20.)

Contents

1	Mountains	1
2	Your Own Hazardous Waste Disposal Problem	11
3	It Helps to Have Heroes	23
4	Where Do I Begin?	29
5	You Can Always Go Home	37
6	Move to the Front Row	45
7	Don't Pass It On	57
8	My Yoke Is Easy	65
9	The Gift of Knowing	75
10	Choices and More Choices	85
11	Being Realistic About Television	95
12	Never Stop Trying	101
	Index	109

I would change my life, O Lord,
But how?
My feet are mired in pathways
Adopted long ago. And days are
Filled with empty tasks
That I must do.

CHAPTER ONE

Mountains

In 1868, a one-armed, thirty-four-year-old geology professor organized an expedition to climb Longs Peak in Colorado. His dream was to see the Colorado River drainage with his own eyes, and to map it for further exploration. Longs Peak is 14,255 feet high, and no one had yet climbed to its summit. All prior attempts to scale it had met with failure. Armed with the experience of others and spurred on by their determined leader, the professor's group succeeded. After much hardship, and without the logistical and technological support which today's climbers enjoy, they finally reached the summit and there celebrated their significant accomplishment. A group member records: "As we were about to leave the summit, Major [John Wesley] Powell [the man responsible for it all] took off his hat and made a little talk. He said, in substance, that we had now accomplished an undertaking in the material or physical field which had hitherto been deemed impossible, but that there were mountains more formidable in other fields of effort which were before us." (L. W. Keplinger, *The Trail,* 1919, quoted in Fred W. Beckey, *Mountains of North America* [San Francisco: Sierra Club Books, 1982], p. 79.)

Speaking of mountains, it is said that the famous philosopher John Dewey, several months before his ninetieth birthday, was questioned about the value of philosophy. "What good is it?" he was asked.

Dewey quietly replied, "The good of it is that you climb mountains."

"Climb mountains?" responded his questioner, unimpressed. "And what's the use of doing that?"

"You see other mountains to climb," was the reply. "You come down, climb the next mountain, and see still others to climb."

Then Dewey said, "When you are no longer interested in climbing mountains to see other mountains to climb, life is over."

I would like to seriously discuss mountains—the "other," more formidable mountains which all of us will have to climb. Life is about metaphorical mountains. Like it or not, they are there, waiting to be climbed. There are mountains of decision, mountains of endurance, mountains of testimony. But one of the most important of all is the mountain of repentance.

Let me share a mountain-climbing experience with you.

Our oldest son has always been interested in heights. When he was a child, and he strayed or got lost, we always looked for him on the highest point of ground we could find. When he was a little older, studying at the university, he wanted an easy course, so he chose a mountain-climbing class. He was hooked for life. The next Christmas he asked for some rope and some carabiners and some clamps and some pitons. It seemed a harmless enough request, and as parents we complied.

It was only natural, I suppose, that the summer before this son left to go on his mission he invited me to go mountain climbing with him. I had always enjoyed the outdoors, and an opportunity to spend some time with him was welcome. I accepted the invitation. But had I known what was in store for me I would not have agreed so readily.

One brilliant fall day we packed a lunch and loaded his equipment in the trunk of the car. We drove up the canyon to Storm Mountain, parked the car, lugged the gear, and went over to the base of a cliff.

He said, "Dad, before you go up this mountain, I want to give you some lessons."

I replied, "Well, I think I have had a little experience with mountains, but I would be happy to listen to whatever you think I ought to know."

So he instructed me how to wrap the rope around me, and how one climber supports another as they both ascend the mountain. He gave me a quick course on how to secure clamps and drive pitons into rocks. In an offhand way he mentioned, "We're doing this so that, if you fall, you won't fall far."

After about ten minutes of instruction, he said: "All right. You know enough. Let's begin by going up that mountain over there." And we did.

As we started up the slope, he said, "Now we can free-climb if you want to, but I recommend that we aid-climb."

I said, "What's the difference?"

He said: "Well, even though this climb isn't too difficult, in either case we'll take precautions. We will drive clamps and secure the climbing rope. If it is a free climb, then we won't use the rope. If it is an aid climb, then *you* may want to use it. If you get into trouble, Dad, just grab the rope. Otherwise, you just go up the mountain and use the rope only if you slip. Don't worry. I will lead the way and show you how it's done."

So he went up the mountain, and I labored up after him. He didn't use the rope at all, and I only used it a time or two. It was steep going as we climbed and struggled. I scraped my knee and slipped a couple of times. Finally, after what seemed like quite a long time, we came out on top of a little ledge about as big as a tabletop. Down one side was a sheer drop of almost two hundred feet. I felt as if I were standing on the roof of a skyscraper, looking over the edge.

He said: "All right, Dad. From here, there are only two ways down. We can go back the way we came, or we can rappel down the face of this cliff."

About that time I wished I had taken a longer course of instruction at the foot of the mountain. I looked apprehensively at the cliff and said, "What do you recommend, son?"

He said, "Well, the reason I came up here was to rappel down this face."

I had read about rock climbers. I had seen them in the movies. Once, long ago in Yosemite Park, I had even watched two intrepid climbers cling to the face of El Capitan. It seemed easy enough. I joked and said, "Straight down certainly looks like the fastest way. Are you sure the rope is long enough?"

4

We threw one end of the rope over the side of the mountain. It was a reinforced, three-hundred-foot climbing rope which would have to be doubled in order for us to successfully descend the face of the cliff. I couldn't see whether it touched the bottom or not, but my nineteen-year-old companion decided that it was "close enough" and that we were ready to go. Then came, as it always does, the moment of truth. We got into a little discussion about who was to go first. "You go first," I said.

He replied, "Well, I'd be happy to go first, Dad, but I think somebody ought to stay up here to help you over the edge."

He was right. I thought about it for a minute and agreed. "Maybe you have a point," I said. "I'll go down first."

Until that moment in my life, mountain climbing had been all fun and games. But as we made a rope harness, and I stepped in it and buckled on some carabiners, I sensed a chill and sober reality in the air. I went over to the edge of the little ledge and prepared myself.

My son said, "Now just step off backwards."

I said, "Not me. I'm going to step off frontwards."

He gently said, "No, you can't do that. What you must do is back over the edge of the cliff, lean on the rope, and when you reach a point where you are at a ninety-degree angle with the face of the rock, then just walk down—as if you were walking backwards on a sidewalk."

I said, "All right, that's what I'll do."

I leaned into the rope and started to back off the cliff. Then I thought, "I can't do this. I really can't."

He sensed my hesitation and said, "You can do it, Dad."

I looked down again and thought to myself, "You shouldn't be doing this, you know. You just might fall. There might be a body lying on those rocks down there. It just might be yours."

Then came another thought. "You know, if my body were down there on those rocks and I were up here, I could see me clear from here."

I looked at my son and said, "I can't do this. I really can't."

There was more than a little disappointment in his voice when he replied, "Well, if you can't, it's okay."

I looked at him and I looked at the rocks below. There was more at stake here than just mountain climbing. He had taught me all he knew. He had assured me that there was no significant danger. I knew that my relationship with him and my image in his eyes were in jeopardy.

I felt as Isaac might have felt when he looked into Abraham's eyes over a stone altar. And at that moment I learned a little bit more about faith and trust. I learned that there are things more important than selfish desires or personal comfort.

I decided I would do it. I said a silent prayer and backed over the cliff. Once I got on the face of the mountain it wasn't at all bad. In fact it was exhilarating. I walked down the cliff. When I came to an overhang, I dangled in the air. After what seemed to be a long time, I came to the end of the rope. We had underestimated the height of the cliff. The rope really wasn't long enough. I abandoned it and scrambled down the last thirty feet or so of mountain on my hands and knees. I couldn't see my son, but I heard him call down the mountain, "Are you all right?"

I walked out into the flat where I could see him, waved my hand, and yelled back, "Piece of cake!"

There are two important lessons to be learned from this story. The first is that you don't really know anything about mountains until you have climbed them. Until you have skinned your knees upon the rocks and felt the naked fear of backing over the edge of the cliff, you don't really understand mountain climbing. When you have burned blisters in the palms of your hands; when you have experienced the breeze that blows in your face when you are at the high point and every way leads down—then you can claim to know a little about the subject.

It is also difficult to know much about repentance unless you yourself have experienced the process. It is a process. It takes time and effort. There are some real, eternal risks if you don't get it right. You can read about or listen to others talk about it, but that doesn't count for much. The Lord intended that we learn some things by doing them. He said, "My doctrine is not mine, but his that sent me. If any man will do his will, he shall know of the doctrine, whether it be of God, or whether I speak of myself." (John 7:16–17.)

Repentance requires that the experience be your own and not someone else's. You can listen to someone talk about his experience on the mountain. It can sound humorous or exciting or easy. But the truth is that there is no way for you to know what it is like unless you go there. There is not a way to get experience without effort. We must earn experiences to make them our own. Sooner or later the important things like faith and testimony—and especially repentance—must be earned, or we run the risk of having them fail us in a time of need. Mortal probation is like that. That is just the way it is.

Once you have climbed the mountain, however, you know it. It is yours. No one can take it away from you. You can then understand how the Prophet Joseph Smith could say, "For I had seen a vision; I knew it, and I knew that God knew it, and I could not deny it, neither dared I do it" (Joseph Smith—History 1:25).

Repentance is a lot like the mountain. We spend a lot of time talking about it in Sunday School or seminary. We listen (but not too well) when the subject is presented to us by those who have walked the way before. We study about it a little. We may even memorize some of the "R's" of repentance, such as Recognition, Remorse, Restitution, Replacement (of bad habits or things lost or damaged), and the Resolve to never repeat the sin. We may understand that we need to confess some things to the bishop. But in spite of all of this, there is never enough instruction at the bottom of the mountain for us to avoid the climb. The experience is not ours until we do it. The real lessons about repentance are those we learn along our own way.

There is another lesson to be learned from mountains: You reach a point where you have to decide which way to go down. You either go down one way or another. There are real consequences associated with each choice. Life, faith, health, and well-being depend on which route we choose.

I mentioned my experience with my son. There was some danger in rappelling down that cliff. Things could have gone wrong. The rope could have broken or the moorings fixed by my teenage son could have failed. There were some risks on the original trail, too; I could have slipped and fallen on my way back that way. But we had reached a point where there were only two things to do. We had to accept the risks and move on; either go over the cliff, or return by the way we came.

There were other things at issue that day as well. My relationship with my son was at stake. I wanted him to be as proud of me as I was of him. I confess that I wanted his respect and his approval. I wondered if I could keep his friendship and trust if I refused his challenge or if I cast doubt on his ability to anchor me on the cliff.

As these thoughts flashed across my mind, I realized that there comes a time when all the theory and all the instruction are put to the test. When all the pros and cons have been weighed and you are alone with your mountain, you have to decide whether you want to climb it or not. You choose, with your own agency, whether it is worth the effort or the embarrassment, whether it is important enough to take the risk. You have to decide whether there is an easier or safer way to reach your objective, or whether honor or trust—or life itself—is worth the price you must pay.

On the mountain that day I decided what I must do. It took a few minutes, but once the decision was made it wasn't too difficult to walk down the cliff.

A mountain is defined as "a natural elevation of the earth's surface, rising abruptly to a summit . . . a large mass . . . a formidable obstacle." This being true, then one doesn't have to be clairvoyant to see that there are metaphorical mountains ahead for each of us: missions, marriage, sickness, death, Church callings, discouragements, even prosperity. These are all mountains—challenges requiring effort to overcome. They may be viewed as new terrain which will bring choices and hazards, both physical and spiritual.

There are trials and temptations on mountains. We may take the wrong course. We may slip and fall.

The effect of a fall from a spiritual mountain can be just as fatal as a fall from an ordinary one. The temptation to take the easy way down will always be present. There will be many who will take off their climbing boots and say, "Well, I never wanted to go mountain climbing in the first place." The truthful reply to them is that no one can avoid the test. We really were put on earth to climb mountains—figuratively, at least. One of the most difficult is the mountain of repentance. Whether we want to climb it or not, our own individual salvation depends on how well we do it.

Resolve is new but ebbs away.
Tomorrow?
Those selfsame tasks and walkways
Are sufficient unto it as well
And leave no time or place for what
The Spirit asks.

CHAPTER TWO

Your Own Hazardous Waste Disposal Problem

Lately we have heard a lot about hazardous waste disposal, about old tailings plants whose sites are radioactive and have the potential to poison anyone, or anything, living near them. We read about nerve gas bombs which are unwanted. They leak and cost more to dispose of than to keep. Some have suggested underground nuclear waste disposal, and we are aware of the controversy surrounding proposals to store these materials in salt mines or deep under the public lands of the West.

Have you ever noticed that much of what contaminates is never destroyed? It just moves from one place to another. No one wants it. And there are costly and difficult decisions to make when someone tries to dispose of it.

My eleven-year-old son wrote to the president of the United States suggesting that contaminated waste be put on board an obsolete rocket and sent to the sun for disposal. So far we've received no reply from the White House. His is one of the best solutions I have heard, but there are those who would say it is too expensive.

Many of us have a similar problem in our personal lives. We feel a need to get rid of some undesirable attribute or bad habit. It is a difficult and time-consuming process. There is no convenient dumping ground. No one steps forward to take our problems from us. Is this not similar to the challenge of disposing of dangerous substances? How do you get rid of things that are hazardous to your salvation?

Perhaps the question could be phrased another way. Assuming a person really wanted to change, how would he or she go about it? I'm not asking how to get someone else to change. That is what Mark Twain had in mind when he wrote, with his pointed humor, "To be good is noble; but to show others how to be good is nobler and no trouble" (Mark Twain, "Pudd'nhead Wilson's New Calendar," in *Everyone's Mark Twain*, comp. C.T. Harnsberger [New York: A.S. Barnes and Co., 1972], p. 219).

But I am not talking about the easier process of showing others how to change. What I mean is that each of us has skeletons in a spiritual closet that would be better disposed of. How would you go about getting rid of one of these if you really wanted to? It isn't easy.

My wife's uncle was a character. They broke the mold, or at least cracked it a little, when they made him. He was colorful and outspoken. He lived on a small farm, a non-Mormon German immigrant in a rural Mormon community. He raised alfalfa and sold honey. As he grew older he leased most of his land to others and spent much of his time watching television. But he kept his bees.

Over the years he resisted the best efforts of the community to convert him to the gospel. He received the Church magazines. Home teachers were assigned to him. He was given countless copies of the Book of Mormon. The stake president even asked him to speak in stake conference once. He accepted, and in his short speech told the members of the stake that he loved them and appreciated how comfortable they made him feel living among them.

We tried to convert him through our love. My wife wrote to him regularly. He was invited to family reunions. In the fall, he and I would go pheasant hunting together. We talked a lot. He was proud of me and followed my accomplishments. It gave him a certain status in his little town to be able to say that his nephew was a General Authority.

He never forgot a kindness. Even though he didn't have much, he shared what he had. Once or twice a year, he would deliver a small can of clear, sweet alfalfa honey to his friends and benefactors.

And with the honey he sent to us came a problem. It came in a coffee can—bright and clean, but a coffee can, nonetheless. You may not have realized it, but a coffee can in a General Authority's kitchen requires a lot of explanations. How do you explain it to the visiting teachers? How do you explain it to the bishop, or to your mother-in-law?

We decided to melt the honey and put it in less controversial containers. But then we realized that even the garbage man knew I was a General Authority. What would he think if an empty coffee can turned up in our trash? Should we talk to him and tell him the truth, or just let him think what he wanted? We even discussed putting the cans in our neighbors' garbage, but, as they were faithful members of the Church, it just didn't seem the right thing to do. It was difficult for us to get rid of those cans.

In a like manner we try to rid ourselves of attributes and habits that could imperil our salvation: for example, immoral actions; spiritually degrading habits; improper thoughts; drug or substance abuse; taking the Lord's name in vain; and procrastination of things we know we should do, such as serving a mission or doing temple work for our ancestors.

Most people know that these things are not good. They wish they were gone from their lives, and yet too often they remain. Like the coffee can, they are not easy to get rid of.

I have a young friend. For some years he has struggled with a serious personal problem. He would do anything to rid himself of it. He feels that he must, because he knows the gospel is true and he knows that if he doesn't his exaltation is in jeopardy. Nevertheless, he often finds temptation at his doorstep and he has, on occasion, opened the door to receive it. Once he asked me if it would be possible for him to receive a priesthood blessing that would take away his desire to sin. He said: "Certainly the priesthood has power to heal me of this torment. Why don't you take my desire to sin from me?"

How would you have answered? Can a priesthood blessing rid us of temptation and sin if we have improper thoughts, degrading habits, or friends that drag us down? Can drug addiction or immorality be erased by simply waving a magic wand? Can the laying on of hands help? Is there an easy way to get rid of such problems in our lives? I think not. They are a little like the coffee cans I referred to earlier. They are hard to dispose of. To do so requires ingenuity and effort. The Lord intended it that way. People who think otherwise remind me of the missionary in a foreign land who once wrote: "President, do you know of a quick way to memorize the discussions? If you do, please send it to me right away."

The only solution to the problem has been given by the Lord. To dispose of sin and bad habits requires that we change and become different people. This lesson the Savior tried to teach Nicodemus. You will remember that Jesus had said, "Except a man be born again, he cannot see the kingdom of God."

Nicodemus then asked, "How can a man be born when he is old? Can he enter the second time into his mother's womb, and be born?" (John 3:3–4.)

Nicodemus just didn't want to understand. Like Laman and Lemuel, he had been told hard things which were more than he could bear (see 1 Nephi 16:1). The only way we can get rid of some of the things in our lives that we do not like is to become different; to think and to act differently; to change habits and to leave old ways behind; to put off the old man and take up the new (see Ephesians 4:24).

So far, though, we have merely defined the problem: a few things should be put behind. Now, how to go about it? What is the first step?

First, you have to want to change. This means more than just thinking that it would be nice to change; or saying, "Someday I will." It means doing more than merely praying, "Lord, take this burden from me." In order to really clean skeletons out of closets, we have to be willing to do something now— like cutting off a hand!

You will recall that on several occasions the Savior

spoke of cutting off a hand or foot or plucking out an eye. He said, "It is better for thee to enter into life halt or maimed, rather than having two hands or feet to be cast into everlasting fire" (Matthew 18:8).

Now I don't think He really meant to cut off a hand at any offense. I think He meant that it is sometimes necessary to take dramatic action to rid ourselves of sin. Sometimes there is no other way. We just have to do things like

1. Move or run away—not from home, but from temptation. Remember that not all those who run from trouble are cowardly—some are brave!
2. Ask friends to help. Make an agreement with them in which they promise to help you change. Even offer to pay them.
3. Change friends or jobs. Dump your boyfriend. Sell your truck.
4. Make a list of ten things (not just one) that you would like to change about your life, and work on all of them at once.
5. Keep a journal. Write your best ideas. Record your progress. Write anything. Whatever you want to put in it is your business; only do it, and do it at a fixed time every day.
6. Do something consciously and intentionally for someone else every day. There is transforming power in service to others.
7. Cut your TV watching in half, and resolve to watch only programs you have selected in advance.
8. Study the scriptures every day. Read them out loud to yourself if you have trouble staying awake. Try not to view the experience just

in terms of chapters or pages but try to make
the scriptures live, as if you were there giving
or hearing the words.
9. Get up at the same time every day. Buy an
alarm clock and use it. Never let an exception
occur, regardless of when you go to bed.
10. Call your bishop. That *would* be dramatic.
Sometimes great loads can be left in his office, never to be carried again.

These ideas really work. Let me share an experience from my own life. When I was first called to be a
stake president, I took a personal inventory. I tried to
find the things in my life which were not consistent
with what I thought a stake president ought to do or
say. I resolved to rid myself of these things so that I
could be more effective and better bless the lives of
the members of my stake. One of the many idiosyn-
crasies I had at that time was the habit of saying, *yeah.*
When people called me on the phone to ask a question, I would say yeah. I found that I was saying it, almost unconsciously, in high council meetings, stake
conferences, and other places. It didn't seem to fit my
image of a stake president, so I resolved to quit.

But I found that I couldn't. As much as I wanted
to avoid it, I heard myself saying yeah in response to
many things. I said yeah at funerals. I said yeah when
talking to the General Authorities. I said yeah when
my children asked me questions. It seemed as if all
the willpower in the world didn't help, and that I was
bound to go to the grave with that word. I could even
imagine the Lord asking me if I wanted to enter the
celestial kingdom and my answering Him, "Yeah."

One day it occurred to me that I needed help. As
I said, this is one of the first steps toward ridding our-

17

selves of many of our undesirable habits. I told my children that I would pay them a quarter for every time they heard me say the word out loud, and that they could collect—on the spot—by merely holding out a hand and saying, "You owe me." In those days, a quarter was worth more than it is now, and my children were young. They accepted the challenge with enthusiasm. They began to follow me around. I would look down from talking on the phone, and one of them would be there with one hand outstretched to receive the money and the fingers of the other hand listing the number of quarters I owed. We could be entertaining guests long after the children were supposed to be in bed, when, out of the darkened hallway, I would see a hand and then hear a small voice say, "You owe me."

I was embarrassed. I got angry. I begged them to have mercy. They thought they had a guaranteed annual income far in excess of any allowance I might have offered them. But, for less than fifty dollars, and with their help, I broke the habit. I never use that word anymore—unless I consciously choose to do so for a worthy purpose. Was it worth it? I should say it was.

I think this is what the Savior meant when He said to cut off your arm. He meant that we should do something to change the negative patterns of life.

Getting rid of things that are hazardous to our salvation isn't easy. It often requires fundamental changes in our lives. It may take time to replace old habits with new ones. It requires discipline and a correct vision of who we are and why we are here.

One of my favorite stories about change and vision has to do with Saul. When he was a boy, living with his father, they one day lost their donkeys. Saul's father told him, "Take now one of the servants with thee, and arise, go seek the asses."

Saul and the servant went around Mount Ephraim and couldn't find them. They went into the land of Shalim. They were not there either. They went to the land of the Benjamites, and they weren't there. They searched everywhere, but without success. Finally, the faithful servant said, "Come, and let us return; lest thy father leave caring for the asses, and take thought for us."

Then they remembered that there was a prophet in the city. The servant had an idea. He suggested, "Peradventure he can shew us our way that we should go."

They decided to go and ask the man of God. On their way they met young maidens going out to draw water. Saul asked them how to reach the prophet's house; and, upon receiving directions, he went up into the city. He could have stopped to talk to the maidens, but he was more interested in finding his animals and going home. He met Samuel. The prophet invited him to stay overnight and said, "To morrow I will let thee go, *and will tell thee all that is in thine heart.* And as for thine asses that were lost three days ago, set not thy mind on them; for they are found. And on whom is all the desire of Israel? Is it not on thee, and on all thy father's house?" (Emphasis added.)

Young Saul was troubled by the prophet's words. He didn't fully understand them. But there were questions in his heart that had nothing to do with the errand he had been given by his father. The prophet had told him that the desire of all Israel was on him. He, like most young men, must have wondered what to do with his life and what he was to be. He found that he was more interested in the answers to these questions than he was even in returning home.

The following day Samuel took the young man with him to offer a sacrifice to the Lord. Afterward he anointed Saul to be a king in Israel, and then sent him on his way. As he did so, he said something remarkable: "When thou art departed from me to day, then thou shalt find two men; . . . and they will say unto thee, The asses which thou wentest to seek are found; and lo, thy father hath left the care of the asses, and sorroweth for you, saying, What shall I do for my son?"

Then Samuel counseled Saul: "Then shalt thou go on forward from thence . . . [and] thou shalt meet a company of prophets. . . . And the Spirit of the Lord will come upon thee, and thou shalt prophesy with them, and shalt be turned into another man."

The scripture tells us that Saul then left Samuel. He encountered all that Samuel had said he would. "God gave him another heart; and all those signs came to pass that day." (See 1 Samuel 9:1–10:9.)

Isn't that what we all need—to get another heart and be turned into another person? The only way to do this is to change, to move out the old and replace it with the new, the right, and the better. It is to not go back to the old ways or to the life where temptation waits.

I started off by talking about your own private hazardous waste disposal problem. Of course, I was really talking about repentance all the time.

Someone asked me once what I thought about repentance. To me, it means that we are given the gift of determining exactly what we are to be judged by, no more and no less. Repentance gives us the privilege and opportunity of approaching the Lord on

Judgment Day, taking with us only those things we are proud of—only our accomplishments, only the good things we have done. We can dispose of everything else, if we want to badly enough; and we will never be judged on the things we have left behind.

Now? O restless waves of conscience
Be still.
My heart is patched with promises.
The conflict rages on. The still
Small voice of "should" cries out—
But I resist.

CHAPTER THREE

It Helps to Have Heroes

In order to change habits, it is helpful to have models. A model enables us to find beauty in a better way. To change for the better requires us to trust and have faith that some of those who live differently have found good reason for doing so. We need to check them out and give their way a trial. A personal model helps us do this and lets us know that change is possible even when we doubt ourselves. A wise man once said:

A society that has no heroes will soon grow enfeebled. Its purposes will be less elevated; its aspirations less challenging; its endeavors less strenuous. Its individual members will also be enfeebled. They will "hang loose" and "lay back" and, so mellowed out, the last thing of which they wish to hear is heroism. They do not want to be told of men and women whose example might disturb them, calling them to effort and duty and sacrifice or even the chance of glory. . . . If we no longer have any heroes, it may not be because no one is fit to be a hero, but because we are not fit to recognize one." (Henry Fairlie, "Too Rich for Heroes," *Harpers*, November 1978, p. 33.)

Most people who live virtuous lives are not uptight or fanatic or narrow. They do not feel compelled to live virtuously; they have deliberately chosen to be free from particular habits. After knowing a lot about the choices, they have carefully chosen not to do or be certain things. Their way brings them peace. If we can model our lives after such individuals, we too can find peace and progress and growth and happiness in this life. Let me tell you about two of my models.

Benjamin Franklin once decided that he knew (or thought he knew) what was right or wrong. He came up with the personal goal of arriving at moral perfection. He said: "I wish'd to live without committing any fault at any time. . . . But I soon found I had undertaken a task of more difficulty than I had imagined." (*Autobiography,* p. 152.)

So Franklin made a list of the virtues he thought he should have in his life. They included temperance, sincerity, moderation, cleanliness, chastity, and humility. It was quite a list. He made a small book in which he allotted a page for each of the virtues. Then he ruled each page with red ink so as to have seven columns, one for each day of the week. He marked each column with a letter for the day. At the end of each day he took inventory, putting a little black spot in the column where he found he had committed a fault against that virtue on that particular day.

He hoped that, by giving strict attention each week to each of the virtues that he wanted to cultivate, he might rid himself of bad habits and so attain perfection.

He decided that he would go through this routine for thirteen weeks—one week for each virtue on his list—and repeat it four times a year. He wrote: "And like him who, having a garden to weed, does not attempt to eradicate all the bad herbs at once, . . . but works on one of the beds at a time, and, having accomplish'd the first, proceeds to a second, so I should have, I hoped, the encouraging pleasure of seeing on my pages the progress I made in virtue . . . till in the end, . . . I should be happy in viewing a clean book" (*Autobiography*, p. 158).

Then he added: "I was surpris'd to find myself so much fuller of faults than I had imagined. But, on the whole, tho' I never arrived at the perfection I had been so ambitious of obtaining, but fell far short of it, yet I was, by the endeavor, a better and a happier man than I otherwise should have been if I had not attempted it." (*Autobiography*, pp. 160–161.)

Franklin's goal was a worthy one. He failed to achieve it. However, it was more important that he made the attempt. Had he had an eternal perspective, he would have realized that the endeavor, or the trying, was more important than he knew. It is the basis of eternal progress. If we try to do better, then sooner or later we *will* be better. If we constantly practice Franklin's pattern, we will eventually qualify for eternal life. Benjamin Franklin is one of my heroes. He taught me to always keep trying.

I met another of my personal heroes when I was a stake president. Our stake basketball team went to the area tournament one year. We had a good team;

and, after some close contests, we found ourselves in the finals, playing for the championship. The contest was a mismatch. The other team had taller, more talented players. As the game progressed, we began to fall behind. We desperately tried to catch up; and in the process, one of our young players fouled the big forward of the other team. It wasn't a deliberate foul, but it wasn't an ordinary foul either. Our 140-pound prospective missionary tripped over his own feet while trying to take the ball away from their 225-pound lean, mean, ex-marine. Sneaker to calf, and elbow to neck, he ran right up the marine's back, driving him headlong into the bleachers at my feet. The boy's momentum carried him to the floor in a heap as well. Trouble was in the making. The marine didn't know what had hit him; but blood was streaming from his nose, and he knew he had been blindsided. He came off the floor with a big fist clenched and murder—or something like it—in his heart.

I had a ringside seat for something that I had never seen in all my years of playing basketball—nor ever since. An experienced referee had been following the play closely. He had seen the foul. He knew how dangerous the situation was and how likely it was that one or both of those young men would very soon be expelled from the game for fighting. He resolved to do something about it.

Talk about cool! Instinctively, he threw himself on the floor between the two players. Majestically sitting between them in his black and white shirt, he did an incredible thing. He folded his arms tightly against his chest, smiled a giant smile, looked directly at the marine, and waited for a blow that never came.

"He fouled you, didn't he?" he said quietly. The big kid nodded his head, menacing the referee with his fist while he tried to refocus on his assailant, who was struggling to his knees, just beyond reach.

"He didn't mean to," said the referee, as he helped the bloodied marine to his feet. "I saw it all. It was an accident. He didn't intend to do it." He put his arm around him and led him gently to the foul line. "Come on," he said. "Let's shoot your foul shots."

The game went on without incident. Our team received the sportsmanship award. A better team won the tournament.

After the contest I spoke to the referee and thanked him. He said, "I didn't do anything special. I just happen to believe that no one should be thrown out of a ball game if I can do anything to prevent it."

That referee and his answer became models for me. They changed my life. They have helped immensely in my ministry. Nobody gets thrown out of the game if I can do anything to prevent it. That's what I mean when I say that to find a model and to live as the model lives is one of the best ways to rid yourself of attributes that are unbecoming to a Latter-day Saint.

If you are fortunate, you will know people like this. Adopt them for your models. If you can't think of any candidates, then use your bishop or the prophet as your examples. Pick some attribute from their lives or some challenge from their teachings, and try to make it part of your life. You will soon sense that you are discovering a better way to live. When this occurs, don't ever turn back. Don't be seduced by the notion that people should accept you for what you are. Tolerant friends will always do that. But if you are not living up to your God-given potential, in the long run you will never be happy.

You may not be fully convinced of your ability to change. But have faith, and trust the Lord. If you do, you will know you are becoming what you should be.

And don't be discouraged if you find that your models are not perfect. Even models struggle, but they keep trying to do better. And that is the secret of just about everything. Almost everyone gets off the strait and narrow path at some time. The real test is what happens next. Is it an excuse to stay off? To enjoy it? Or does such a test provoke diligent effort to pick up the pieces and return to the better way?

What we really need is what Saul needed—another heart. One way to get one is find a better way, to find a model, and then want to change so much that we never go back to what we were. Many others have done it. Why can't we?

Doubt. Resolve. Is there no rest?
And fear,
Unsure of what to do, or when.
Unsheltered from the fray, I
Long for peace but stumble on—bound
To yesterday.

CHAPTER FOUR

Where Do I Begin?

Picture two crystal goblets. They differ in size and shape. They are both of good quality and have been well used. One has been carefully kept in a china cupboard. It is clean and polished, warm and inviting in appearance. It sparkles in the light. It is filled with clear water.

The other glass is coated with grime. It has not been in a dishpan for a long time and has been used for purposes other than those for which it was made. Most recently it has been left outside in the weather and has served as a flowerpot. The flower is gone, but the glass is still filled with dirt. It is dull and unbecoming in the light.

Is not each of us like a crystal glass? We vary in size and shape. Some of us radiate a special spirit.

Others are dull and uninviting. Some fill the measure of their creation. Others do not. Each is filled with the accumulated experiences or debris of a lifetime.

Some contain mostly good things—clean thoughts, faith, and Christian service. These hold wisdom and peace. Others enclose some dark and secret things. Over time they have been filled with unclean thoughts, selfishness, and sloth. They are often filled with doubt, contention, and unrest.

Many know they are not living up to their potential but for various reasons have procrastinated making changes in their lives. Some long for they know not what and spend their lives in a haphazard pursuit of happiness.

Such people are like the crystal goblet which spent part of its existence filled with dirt. They sense that there is a higher purpose to things. They become dissatisfied and begin to search for meaning. First they look outside themselves. They may sample the pleasures of the world. As they do, they discover—much as did the snail who set out to look for its house—that, after arriving at wherever they were going, they are no closer than before to the object of their search.

Ultimately, they look within. They have really known all the time that this was where to search for peace. Sin, you see, is not just a state of mind. Wickedness never was and never will be happiness (see Alma 41:10). They discover that if they are not righteous they can never be happy (see 2 Nephi 2:13). They resolve to change. Then they are confronted, figuratively, with the problem of how to turn a weathered flowerpot into a sparkling crystal goblet. They ask sincere questions: Can I ever be forgiven? Is it really worth the effort? Where do I begin?

In the case of the glass, it is easy to understand what to do. We begin by recognizing a better use for the crystal. A convenient place for dumping the unwanted contents is selected, and the dirt is discarded there. The goblet is carefully washed with high-quality detergent to remove the stains and residue. It is lovingly polished. It is placed once again in the company of other crystal glasses in the china cupboard. Then it is put back into service and cared for regularly.

There is a similar process whereby men and women are purified. Through it, the misuse of their lives is forgotten, and they are renewed and changed. This principle, of course, is repentance. When accompanied by authorized baptism, it provides not only an initial cleansing but also an ongoing remission of sins. Participating in this purifying process is perhaps the most thrilling and important thing we can ever do. It has far-reaching, even eternal, consequences. And there are more immediate rewards: peace and forgiveness in this present life.

Let me illustrate what all of this means. Once when I was a bishop I was asked to speak to a group of young men. I don't remember now exactly what I said except that, near the end of my talk, I made a statement that no one present had done anything for which he could not be forgiven.

After the meeting was over, one of the young men came up to me and said, "I just have to talk to you." Inasmuch as I had another appointment, I asked if it could wait, or if someone else could answer his question. He replied that he had already waited many years and that it was very important to him. So, taking advantage of the few minutes available, we found a little classroom that was not in use, went in, and closed the door.

"Did you really mean it? Did you?" he asked.

"Mean what?" I said.

"The part about how none of us had done anything that could not be forgiven," he replied.

"Of course I did," I said.

Then, through tears, his story came. He had good parents. All of his life his mother had told him he would be going on a mission. But, before he turned nineteen, he had been involved in serious transgression. He didn't know how to tell his parents. He knew it would break their hearts. He did know that he wasn't worthy to serve a mission. In desperation, he began to look for an excuse to avoid that call. He decided to take up smoking. He felt that his father could understand that better and would not probe for the real reason. His smoking would hurt his parents, he rationalized, but not as deeply as his true reason.

He soon found, however, that his former bishop wasn't put off by his use of tobacco. The bishop told him to just stop smoking and go on a mission anyway. So, to get away from the bishop, he entered military service. There he fell under the influence of some good Latter-day Saints. He stopped smoking. He was able to avoid additional major temptations. He served his time in the military, received an honorable discharge, and returned home.

There remained only one major problem. He still felt guilty. He had run away from a mission. He had run from the Lord. He sensed that gnawing discontent which comes when men do not live up to the purpose of their creation.

"So there you have it," he said. "I have not sinned again. I have attended my meetings. I keep the Word of Wisdom. Why is it that life seems empty? Why do I feel somehow that the Lord is displeased with me? How can I know for sure that I have been forgiven?"

"Tell me what you know about repentance," I said.

He had obviously done some reading on the subject. He spoke of recognition, remorse, and restitution. He had resolved to never sin again.

"Let's see just how those principles apply to you," I said. "Let's begin with recognition. What is the best indicator that someone recognizes he has done wrong?"

"He will admit it," was his reply.

"To whom?" I asked.

He was thoughtful. "To himself, I guess."

"Men sometimes view themselves in a most favorable light," I said. "Wouldn't better evidence of awareness of wrongdoing be to tell someone else?"

"Yes, of course," he answered.

"Who else?" I insisted.

"Why, the person wronged," he said, "and . . . maybe the bishop."

"Have you done this?" I asked.

"Not until now," he replied. "I've never told it all to anyone but you."

"Maybe that is why you have not ever felt completely forgiven," I responded. He didn't say much.

"Let's look at the next step," I said. "What does it mean to feel remorse?"

"It means to be sorry," he answered.

"Are you sorry?" I asked.

"Oh yes," he said. "I feel as if I have wasted half my life." And his eyes filled again with tears.

"How sorry should you be?"

He looked puzzled. "What do you mean?"

I said: "Well, in order to be forgiven, a transgressor must experience godly sorrow. He must have

anguish of soul and genuine regret. This sorrow must
be strong enough and last long enough to motivate
the additional processes of repentance; otherwise, it
is not deep enough. Regret must be great enough to
bring forth a changed person. That person must
demonstrate that he is truly changed, by doing different and better things. Have you been sorry enough?"
I asked again.

He hesitated. "I've changed," he said. "I'm not the
same as I was before. I try to keep all the commandments now. I would like to somehow make it up to
my parents. I have prayed for forgiveness. I apolo-
gized to the person I wronged. I realize the seriousness of what I did. I would give anything if it hadn't
happened. I maybe haven't been as good as I could
be, but I don't know what else to do. But I didn't ever
confess to anyone."

I said, "I think after this meeting we can say you
have done even that."

Then he said, "But after all of that, how can I ever
know the Lord has forgiven me?"

"That is the easy part," I replied. "When you have
fully repented, you feel an inner peace. You know you
are somehow forgiven because the burden you have
carried for so long, all of a sudden, isn't there anymore. It is gone, and you know it is gone."

He seemed doubtful still.

"I wouldn't be surprised," I said, "if, when you
leave this room, you discover that you have left much
of your concern in here. If you have fully repented,
the relief and the peace you feel will be so noticeable
that it will be a witness to you that the Lord has forgiven you. If it doesn't happen today, I think it will
happen soon."

I was late for my next meeting. I opened the door,

and we went out together. I didn't know if we would ever meet again.

The following Sunday evening I received a telephone call at my home. It was from the young man. "Bishop, how did you know?"

"How did I know what?" I asked.

"How did you know that I would feel good about myself for the first time in five years?"

"Because the Lord promised He would remember our sins no more," I said.

Then came the question: "Do you think the Church could use a twenty-four-year-old missionary? If they could, I would sure like to go."

That young man was like one of the glasses we spoke about. He had been out in the world and was partially filled with the wrong things. He was not content. Sin had clouded his vision and interfered with his potential. Until he could find a way to repent, he could never become what he knew he should be. It took time to change. It took prayer. It took effort. And it took help.

My young friend discovered that repentance is often a lonely, silent struggle. It is not a once-in-a-lifetime thing; rather it lasts a lifetime. As President Stephen L Richards once said, it is an "ever-recurring acknowledgment of weakness and error and [a] seeking and living for the higher and better" (*Improvement Era*, June 1956, p. 397).

This young man came to know that repentance is not just a free gift. Just as faith without works is dead, so repentance demands works. It is not for the fainthearted or the lazy. It requires a complete turning away from wrongdoing and a set of new works or doings which can produce a new heart and a different man. Repentance means effort. It is not simply stopping doing something. It is not just recognizing the wrong or knowing what should be done. It is not "a cycle of sinning and repenting and sinning again" (Hugh B. Brown, *Eternal Quest*, sel. C. M. Brown [Salt Lake City: Bookcraft, 1956], p. 102).

It is not only remorse. Rather, it is an eternal principle which, when properly applied over sufficient time, always results in renewal, cleansing, and change.

The young man we have spoken about discovered that where sin is so serious as to jeopardize one's fellowship in the Church, the sinner must be willing to submit to the jurisdiction and judgment of the person who holds the custody of his Church membership. He must request forgiveness from him, as the Church's representative, as well as from the offended person.

Most important of all, this man learned that repentance is an indispensable counterpart to free agency. Free agency in the plan of salvation contemplates that men and women are free to choose for themselves the direction of their lives. Repentance means that, since imperfect beings sometimes make imperfect decisions, they may correct their course. By our following the rules of repentance, and through the atonement of Christ, we can come to know that mistakes don't count. The Lord agrees to "remember [our sins] no more" (Hebrews 8:12). Because of the miraculous gift of forgiveness, transgressions are forgiven—and forgotten. Men can be cleansed and can then return to the path of purpose and progress and peace.

By repenting, my young friend became a new person. He was born again of the Spirit. He came to understand for himself (and that is the important thing) the meaning of the Savior's words "Come unto me, all ye that labour and are heavy laden, and I will give you rest" (Matthew 11:28).

What must I do, O Lord, must
Shadows
Of the past forever cloud the day?
What can I say or do, to let my song
Again be heard on that straight but
Shrouded way?

CHAPTER FIVE

You Can Always
Go Home

From the beginning, prophets have called people
to repentance. Those who have not known about the
gospel have been exhorted to abandon their sinful
ways, keep the commandments, and join with the
people of the Lord.

But prophets have also pleaded with another
group—those who were once believers, but who, because of pride or sin or something else, have abandoned the faith. In this group are the less active, the
critics, the uncommitted, and the rebellious. These
are Church members who have grown away from
God. To these, the invitation has always been to
come back to the Lord.

As we think about members of the Church repenting and returning to activity, the stories of Paul

and Alma may come to mind. Some people may be waiting for a miraculous experience similar to theirs before committing themselves again. However, they will probably wait in vain; for, as the Savior taught His disciples, "If they hear not Moses and the prophets, neither will they be persuaded, though one rose from the dead" (Luke 16:31).

Without such a dramatic incentive to change, others may wonder if it is possible to return to faith from doubt. Can the cynic ever really become as a little child? Can the slave of habit or passion become free again? Is there a way back? If so, is it worth the effort to find and follow it? Where and when does one begin?

There *is* a way—for surely prophets do not teach in vain. And just as surely, the Lord hears the prayers of teachers and leaders and parents who pray for the return of those who are lost.

Some may think the way is not clearly marked, for in all of scripture there are recorded but a few instances of former believers ever repenting. Be that as it may, the fact remains that thousands have returned from inactivity. Let me tell you about some who did.

When I was first called to be a bishop, I inherited the stewardship of a large ward. Many of the eight hundred or so members did not come out to church. I had never met the members of that group, so I resolved to do so.

One Sunday afternoon in November, I went to visit an inactive family. As I came up to the house, a woman was sweeping the porch. I introduced myself as the new bishop and asked if her husband was home.

"Yes," she said, "but he won't talk to you. We are tired of being bothered. My husband asked the other bishop to take our names off the records of the Church. We don't want home teachers. We don't want people collecting fast offerings. We just want to be left alone." She changed her grip on the broom. "Now get out," she said, "Get off my porch; get out of my yard; and don't come back." The broom was coming at me, as I backed down the steps. I stammered a few words of apology, which were ignored. "Git," she said. And I did.

I didn't sleep well that night. I had been humiliated. Worse still, it seemed, the office of the bishop had been treated with disrespect. By Tuesday night, I had almost decided that the woman and her husband should be excommunicated. But a wise counselor and a careful reading of instructions from Church headquarters persuaded me otherwise.

After that, I said hello to that family when I occasionally met them on the street. But I never returned to the home. However, we did assign a relative to visit there each month to watch over them. As far as I know, no gospel message was given and no other significant Church contact was made with that family during the years I served as bishop.

After a time, the ward was divided. I was released and was called to be stake president. On another Tuesday night, some years later, one of our bishops came to the stake office and asked if I would be available later in the evening to interview an older couple for a temple recommend. He had been working with them for months, and they were finally ready to go to the temple.

He said, "You may know them, President," and he mentioned the name of the woman with the broom.

I could hardly wait for that interview. At about nine o'clock, the bishop brought to my office a well-dressed elderly couple. He introduced them. I recognized them as the same people I had known before, but they were different somehow. I invited the good sister to come into the office first. I asked her if she knew who I was, and she replied, "Oh yes, you are the stake president."

"Do you remember a Sunday afternoon in November, thirteen years ago?" I asked, "A young bishop came to your door and wanted to know if you and your husband would like to become more active in the Church. Do you remember turning him away?"

"I don't remember anything like that," she said. "I'm sure I would never have done such a thing."

Then I said: "I have another question. Why have you waited so long to come back to the Church?"

"Well, we always knew we would have to get active again someday," she replied. "We wanted to. We just never got around to it. My husband used to smoke a lot, and he didn't feel comfortable going to church. I prayed for years that he would quit. Then, when he started to have health problems a couple of years ago, it seemed like a good time to go back."

I finished the interview and talked with her husband as well. They were now completely worthy. Shortly thereafter, they went to the temple to be sealed.

Notice the elements of their return: It wasn't easy. They had always known. She had prayed for years. There was a lot of wasted time. Finally, before it was too late, they talked to the bishop, repentance took place, old attitudes and habits were forgotten, and they came back.

Another who came back was Aminadab. He had once belonged to the church of God, but he had become critical and contentious. He evidently sympathized with the opposition. He was among the party which went to the jail to get two young missionaries, Nephi and Lehi, who were being held captive there. They intended to kill the two men.

But a cloud of darkness came upon them, and they heard a still, mild voice whisper, "Repent, . . . and seek no more to destroy my servants." Surprised, Aminadab turned around and looked at Nephi and Lehi. Their faces shone through the darkness, and they appeared to be lifting their eyes and their voices to someone in heaven.

Aminadab then recognized them as servants of God. In a loud voice he told the other Lamanites and dissenters in the group to turn and look. As they did, they too were given power to see the faces of Nephi and Lehi through the darkness which surrounded them. They asked Aminadab how to dispel the cloud of darkness; and he, drawing on truth I believe he had learned at another time, said: "You must repent, and cry unto the voice [of the Lord], even until ye shall have faith in Christ; . . . and when ye shall do this, the cloud of darkness shall be removed from overshadowing you." (See Helaman 5:21–52.)

Now notice again: the scripture speaks of darkness overshadowing those who have abandoned the faith. The effect of darkness is to prevent one from seeing clearly. To find the way back, as Aminadab discovered, one must repent and pray, until doubt and darkness disappear and important things can be seen again.

One final story—once again from the period when I was a bishop. One night, while I was in a sound sleep, the doorbell rang. I stumbled to answer it and found a young member of my priests quorum at the door. I knew him well—well enough to have gone on outings with him, to have prayed with and about him, and to have taught him. I knew him as well as a good bishop knows any active eighteen-year-old priest, which was well enough for me to anxiously ask what he was doing at my front door in the middle of the night.

He said, "I have to talk to you, Bishop. I've just done something serious, and I can't go home."

He was right. It was serious. I invited him in, and we talked. He talked, and I listened; then I talked, and he listened, until dawn. He had many questions. He had committed a terrible sin. He wanted to know if there was hope. He wanted to know how to repent. He wanted to know if repentance included telling his parents. He wanted to know if there was any chance of his going on a mission. He wanted to know many other things.

I didn't have all the answers, but I told him there was hope. I told him that coming back would be difficult, but it was possible. I explained what I knew about the process of repentance, and I helped him to determine what he must do. I told him that if he really wanted to go on a mission, that decision could be made only in the future, after he had repented. Then I told him to go home, and he did.

He made his peace with his parents. He asked forgiveness from those he had wronged. He put sin and bad company behind him and did everything he could to repent.

A year or so later, five young men from that quorum went on missions. He was one of them. I was close to them all. I attended each of their farewell services. They all served honorable missions. Within a brief time after returning home, they each married in the temple. My wife and I attended each of the wed-

ding ceremonies. Even today, I could take a piece of
paper and write on it their names and the names of
their wives and some of their children. That is how
well I knew them.

But now let me tell you something—something
very private and very important. *I cannot remember* the
name of the young man who came to my home in the
middle of the night. I know he was one of the five,
but I don't remember which one.

There was a time when I worried about that. I
thought perhaps my memory might be failing. I consciously tried to recall who had had the problem, but
I could not.

I was eventually released as a bishop, and I put
the entire incident out of my mind. On a late evening
walk some years later, I found myself in the ward
where I had once been bishop. The shadowy quiet
brought back many memories. I was deep in thought
when I realized I was walking in front of a house
where one of my priests had lived years before. Suddenly, the story of the young man I had mentioned
came to mind, and I tried to remember which of the
five he had been. Had he lived in that house? Why
couldn't I remember?

As I continued on my way, something happened—
something difficult to explain, but real to me. I seemed
to hear a voice which said: "Don't you understand, my
son? I have forgotten that. Why should you remember?"

I was chagrined. There was no justifiable response
to that question. I have never wondered about it
again. And I knew more surely then than I had ever
known before, that the Lord is pleased when His children return to Him.

All who are shepherds and all who are lost sheep
should note this one last thing: The Lord really meant

it when He said, "He who has repented of his sins, the same is forgiven, and I, the Lord, remember them no more" (D&C 58:42).

Some years ago, it was fashionable in certain circles to use the phrase, "You can never go home again." That is simply not true. It *is* possible to return. It is possible for those who have ceased to pray to pray again. It is possible for those who are lost to find their way through the dark and to come home. And when they do, they will know, as I know, that the Lord is more concerned with what a person is than with what he was, and with where he is than with where he has been.

And so I cried, until at last
An answer
Came—clear, and familiar too.
It was not the first time I had
Heard the words, though they were
Strangely new.

CHAPTER SIX

Move to the Front Row

In my observation there are three kinds of members of the Church: Members who are anxiously engaged; those who are willing; and those who are reluctant or unwilling. You can generally tell which is which by where they sit in church. The anxiously engaged members sit in front. The willing members sit anywhere they can find a seat. (However, inasmuch as they have many things to do, they don't always arrive at meetings early; therefore they don't sit in the seats of the anxiously engaged.) The reluctant members never sit in front. They prefer the back row, literally and figuratively.

The anxiously engaged want to be identified with the work. They want to hear the speaker, to feel the Spirit, and to be an integral part of what is going on.

The willing constitute the backbone of the Church. They are believers, but they are often busy with other things as well. They have families, school, social life, political or community activities. All of these things compete for the time and attention of the willing, who sometimes wait for a calling in the Church before they do much. It was to this group that the Lord gave this counsel: "Men should be anxiously engaged in a good cause and do many things of their own free will, and bring to pass much righteousness; for the power is in them wherein they are agents unto themselves. . . . But he that doeth not anything until he is commanded, and receiveth a commandment with doubtful heart, and keepeth it with slothfulness, the same is damned." (D&C 58:27–29.)

Unwilling or reluctant members are those who are afraid the gospel might be true. They come to church because of others: perhaps for girlfriends, parents, teachers, and so forth. They are not fully repentant, they do not let the Spirit guide their lives; but they are yet drawn to the Church by forces they do not completely comprehend.

It is dangerous to oversimplify things, such as the reasons why people sit where they sit in church. Nevertheless, to provoke thought, let me suggest that most people who come to church can be divided into two groups: front-row members and back-row members.

At a stake conference I attended sometime ago the stake center was filled with chairs. The stake president asked that I speak to his young people before the general session. I agreed. Some two hundred and fifty of them came to a sunrise service at eight o'clock. They sat in widely scattered locations throughout the chapel and cultural hall. The not-yet-awake priests and teachers sat in the overflow area just outside of the chapel. Couples that were dating sat together in the four corners of the building or in the middle of the cultural hall. A few little girls in long dresses sat near the front.

It was almost as if they thought I had a communicable disease. No one wanted to take a chance on catching what I had. There was some real reason for concern in this regard, I suppose, because the gospel is highly contagious if you are exposed to it long enough, or if it is handled with enthusiasm. The question came to my mind then and merits attention now, why is it that almost no one at most church gatherings wants to appear really involved in what is going on? Putting the question another way—why do many young people in the Church want to be back-row members?

As I have thought about that question, I have come up with some answers. I have concluded that there are fourteen reasons why some of us choose the last rows in church. Those rows provide a good place

1. To talk, read, or sleep.
2. To be with friends who also want to talk, read, or sleep.
3. To slip into a meeting late.
4. To leave early.
5. To escape being called on.
6. To be unnoticed when we don't take the sacrament.
7. To avoid getting trampled on in case of fire or earthquake.
8. To get out of the parking lot before the crowd.
9. To keep from getting involved.
10. To put as much distance as possible from the speaker and what is going on; and thereby to

build barriers of noise and space between ourselves and the Spirit.

11. To not appear too anxiously engaged.
12. To join the spectator group.
13. To maintain our standing as critics-in-residence and continue to serve the Lord in an advisory capacity.
14. To find a seat when there are no others available. (This last excuse is the only one of the foregoing that I find justifiable. However, such a case many be more theoretical than factual. The back seats in church always fill up much sooner than the others.)

I used to be a lawyer. My time and my talent were devoted to the cases or causes of my clients. Whatever skill, brainpower, and ability I had were for sale, so to speak. I specialized in appellate matters, often arguing cases before the courts of appeal or the supreme court. The largest case I ever dealt with involved some fifteen million dollars. After hundreds of hours of effort, my client and I obtained a successful decision from the Supreme Court of the United States. My client got the fifteen million dollars. I was accorded a footnote in history as counsel of record in that great case. It couldn't have been won without believing in the cause; without involvement, study, enthusiasm, and anxious concern for every aspect of the law and every detail of fact.

You know, the gospel is more important than all of that. In my experience the gospel is the only totally worthwhile cause in all the world. If it is not worth everything—and I really mean everything—it is worth nothing, nothing at all.

That is why it is so distressing to me to see members of the Church, both young and old, approach the gospel so diffidently. Too many are restrained and reserved in manner and attitude about the most important thing in all the world. This lack of enthusiasm about the good news for which Jesus Christ gave His life is most prevalent among back-row Mormons. I have a confession to make: nothing bothers me quite so much as such "Joe Cool" members of the Church.

If the prophet were in our sacrament meeting today, where would we want to be? Would we want as much distance between him and us as possible? Or would we want to draw near, to touch him, to feel his spirit, and to see his soul?

What if the Savior were here? Would we feel the same? Would we want to be near Him or far away? Would we go to meet Him, or would we wait for Him to come to meet us? I sometimes think that it will take something as catastrophic as the Millennium to get the attention of the back-row crowd.

You know, we have an unfortunate habit in the Church of thinking in terms of *we* and *they*, rather than *us*. Often *we* are the back-row boys. *They* are those who live the gospel. We hear such things as, "They (the Brethren, parents, institute teachers, the stake, etc.) don't understand us." "They (the Church) should do this." "They (the home teachers) don't meet our needs." "If they (the members) had only done their jobs in missionary work, I would have had a good mission." And on and on. Everywhere we go, we hear these or similar things. All are echoed by those on the figurative back row.

It is said that there is nothing so easy but that it becomes difficult when done with reluctance. The back-row member is reluctant to pray, to keep commandments, to serve, to do. Some of these things are not particularly easy to do anyway, even with enthusiasm; but when approached with reluctance, they become impossible. Few leaders of the Church are called from the back row. A young girl would be a fool to choose a future husband from the back row. Pity the child whose father is comfortable on the back row. This is because, as William James once said, "The best way to define a man's character is to seek out the particular mental or moral attitude in which he [feels] himself most deeply and intensely active and alive. At such moments there is a voice inside which speaks and says: 'This is the real me.'"

Thus, if the mental and moral attitudes which I have attributed to the back row are those which bring a sense of belonging to a member of the Church, then those are the attitudes which define our character, at least until a dramatic change of heart takes place.

As the Savior prepared to leave His twelve Nephite disciples, He called them together for some final intimate counsel. He told them He had come into the world to do the will of His Father, because His Father had sent Him. Then He said: "Ye know the things that ye must do in my church; for the works which ye have seen me do that shall ye also do; for that which ye have seen me do even that shall ye do" (3 Nephi 27:21).

Then came the provocative question, "Therefore what manner of men ought ye to be?" (3 Nephi 27:27).

Intending no disrespect and with utmost reverence, I have imagined myself as a backsliding member of the Church, having such a conversation with the Savior. Just the two of us alone. In my imaginings, I was searching for spiritual identity, trying to discover who I really was, what my place in life was, what manner of man I ought to be. The question of whether or not I should change my life, whether I should give up my season ticket on the back row and move to the front row, came into discussion. Here is that imaginary conversation. The questions are mine. Note that the answers are really His, as provided to us through the scriptures.

"Lord," I said, from my comfortable back-row seat, "why can't I go through life just as I am?"

He answered, "You have many things to do and to repent of: for behold, your sins have come up unto me, and are not pardoned, because you seek to counsel in your own ways" (D&C 56:14). "Thou shalt not idle away thy time, neither shalt thou bury thy talent that it may not be known" (D&C 60:13).

"But," I continued, in my imagination, "if I move to the front row, I'll have to pay tithing, and I may even have to sell my sports car."

He said, "Thou shalt not covet thine own property" (D&C 19:26). "Lay aside the things of this world, and seek for the things of a better" (D&C 25:10).

"But they dress so funny on the front row," I said. "White shirts, short hair, ties, and all of that."

He said, "Thou shalt not be proud in thy heart; let all thy garments be plain" (D&C 42:40).

I said, "They don't appear to have much fun on the front row, Lord."

He said, "Let the solemnities of eternity rest upon your mind" (D&C 43:34). "Cast away your idle thoughts and your excess of laughter far from you. . . . Cease from all your light speeches, . . . from all your lustful desires, from all your pride and light-mindedness, and from all your wicked doings. Cease to be idle; . . . cease to sleep longer than is needful; retire to thy bed early, that ye may not be weary; arise early, that your body and your mind may be invigorated. And above all things, clothe yourself with the bond of charity, as with a mantle, which is the bond of perfectness and peace." (D&C 88:69, 121, 124–125.)

"But the girls (or the guys) are so plain on the front row," I said.

He replied, "He that looketh on a woman to lust after her . . . shall not have the Spirit, but shall deny the faith and shall fear" (D&C 63:16).

And then He said, "Favour is deceitful, and beauty is vain: but a woman that feareth the Lord, she shall be praised" (Proverbs 31:30).

I said: "What about my friends on the back row? They'll make fun of me."

He said, "Repent, . . . for [thou] seeketh the praise of the world" (D&C 58:39). "For whoso cometh not unto me is under the bondage of sin. And whoso receiveth not my voice is not acquainted with my voice, and is not of me. And by this you may know the righteous from the wicked." (D&C 84:50–53.)

I said, "Okay, okay. But will I have to go on a mission?"

He said, "The thing which will be of the most worth unto you will be to declare repentance unto this people, that you may bring souls unto me" (D&C 15:6). "Unto what were ye ordained? To preach my gospel by the Spirit, even the Comforter which was sent forth to teach the truth." (D&C 50:13–14.)

"Well," I said, "I know I should. But can I have just a little fun first?"

He replied, "He that seeketh me early shall find me, and shall not be forsaken" (D&C 88:83).

"I'm not sure I'll ever feel comfortable on the front row," I said hesitantly.

He replied, "Be of good cheer, for I will lead you along" (D&C 78:18). "Be ye strong" (D&C 38:15). "Do these things . . . with a glad heart" (D&C 59:15). "Therefore walk with me" (Moses 6:34). "Learn that he who doeth the works of righteousness shall receive his reward, even peace in this world, and eternal life in the world to come" (D&C 59:23).

"But why can't I do all that without moving to the front row?" I persisted.

He answered, as I knew He would: "Verily I say, men should be *anxiously* engaged in a good cause, and do many things of their own free will, and bring to pass much righteousness; for the power is in them, wherein they are agents unto themselves" (D&C 58:27–28, emphasis added).

Then He said, "Behold, this is my work and my glory—to bring to pass the immortality and eternal life of man" (Moses 1:39).

"All right," I said, "you've convinced me. Where do I go from here?"

He answered: "Shall we not go on in so great a cause? Go forward and not backward." (D&C 128:22.) "Forsake the world" (D&C 53:2). "Lift up your heart and rejoice, . . . and take upon you my whole armor, that ye may be able to withstand the evil day, having done all" (D&C 27:15).

The Savior, through the scriptures, will answer any questions which affect your eternal salvation. I have tried to dramatize some of the answers to some of those questions through my imaginary conversation with Him.

I personally know a little about the back row. When I was a young man, I left home to go to college. Moving to a strange city, I rented an apartment which was off campus and in a downtown ward. No one there worried about my church attendance, and no one at the institute was particularly concerned about me either. I remember vividly one Sunday afternoon, more than thirty years ago, when I was driving down the boulevard with a friend. It was nearly three o'clock in the afternoon. We had no plans. The thought crossed our minds that we might go to a movie. As we drove, I heard in my mind the whispering of the Spirit, which said to me, "Go to the institute to church. You are needed there." I have heard that voice many times since and I have learned to react with more speed and grace than I did that day. But on that afternoon, I mentioned to my friend that I had a funny feeling that perhaps we should go to church. To show you how far on the back row we were, he said, "All right, I guess the one is about as good as another. If you feel that way, let's do it." We turned the car around, drove back to the institute parking lot, left the car, and entered the door of the old chapel at about two minutes to three.

The institute director, Brother W. W. Richards, was at the door, shaking hands with latecomers. When he saw me approaching, he said: "Burt, I have been standing here trying to find someone to offer the opening prayer. I believe that you could add a significant dimension to our sacrament meeting if you would do that. Will you?" I said yes. He escorted me to the stand. I said the prayer. I don't remember anything else about the meeting. I don't even remember the prayer. But I do remember a near-miraculous series of events which began that day and caused me to move from the back row slowly, imperceptibly perhaps, into the mainstream of activity in the Church.

The attitudes of the back row are in us all. As we grow older it doesn't get any easier to support the

Church and to be loyal and faithful. Little things, such as the Word of Wisdom, tithing, a quarrel with a neighbor, Church assignments, or the lack of them, can keep us from the only institution that can really help us to become what we should be. Because we seem to see imperfections in the Church, we sometimes tend to be hesitant about wholeheartedly becoming one with it. The danger in being apart from it is that we will not gain the spiritual strength which always comes from the Church; as a result, sin can enter our lives. Sin brings with it rationalization; rationalization excludes repentance; and sin without repentance is spiritual death.

On the inside cover of an *Ensign* magazine a few years ago appeared a little poem called "Awakening."

Oh, Lord, I have been a slothful servant,
Doing Thy will reluctantly, only at Thy bidding,
And hiding behind a pillar
In hopes Thou would not see
And so—not command.

I do not know what wind
Blew the scales from my eyes
So that suddenly I began to see
What miracles lay even within my poor grasp.
I do not know when reluctance turned to willingness,
And willingness to the eagerness of joy in Thy work.
What wasted years! Oh, God!
I was not free until I loosed the shackles of my
    selfishness
And accepted the greatest gift Thou had to give me
    in this life—
Service.

— *Dorris Riter*

One last word. In a sacrament meeting in my home ward, approximately one year before I was called to be a General Authority, I was thinking about the course of my life and what I might best do to find fulfillment, happiness, and success. I heard the still small voice in my mind again. I wrote the message down, because that kind of an experience doesn't happen every day. The Spirit said, "The most important thing in your life right now is to chart the course from where you are to where you want to be, and then to put your whole effort into getting where you should be, as soon as you can, before it is too late."

"Begin again," the Spirit said,
"Ere day
Turns into day. As you once learned
To whistle, by wanting to,
Pursing childish lips till first faint
Music came,

CHAPTER SEVEN

Don't Pass It On

In a schoolyard game young boys sometimes form a circle, and one hits another on the shoulder and says, "Pass it on." The one who receives the blow obediently transmits it to the next in line and says, "Pass it on." The third recipient promptly punches a fourth, and each in succession thereafter "passes it on," trying to reduce his own pain, and the responsibility for it, by inflicting it on another.

Many of us are like these schoolboys. Sometimes without realizing it we continue to play the same childish game; but we risk far more than a bruised shoulder. Let me explain what I mean.

Unwillingness to accept responsibility for and consequences of one's actions is an all-too-common condition in today's world. Who has not heard of the drunken driver who sues his host for allowing him to get drunk, or of the accident victim who claims damages from the physician who had offered help? Perpetrators of the most heinous crimes often plead guilty by reason of insanity, or claim that they are victims of society's ills. Homeless people sometimes blame alcohol for their problems. Alcoholics blame genetic deficiencies. Abusers and adulterers blame the broken homes of their childhood. And there are enough who agree with them to ensure that they needn't feel terribly guilty for long if they don't want to.

The habit of shifting the burden of guilt to someone else, while perhaps understandable in a secular setting, has more serious consequences in a spiritual one. There too it has an ancient, though not honorable, tradition.

Cain blamed God when his sacrifice was not accepted. "I was wroth," he said, "for his offering thou didst accept and not mine" (Moses 5:38).

Laman and Lemuel blamed Nephi for nearly all their troubles (see 1 Nephi 16:18, 36). Pilate blamed the Jews when he condoned the crucifixion of Jesus, in whom he found "no fault" (see John 19:4, 6).

Even the very elite have sometimes succumbed to the temptation to blame others for their disobedience or their failure to receive blessings. Aaron blamed the children of Israel when Moses charged him with bringing a great sin upon them by making a molten calf (see Exodus 32:21–24). And Martha may have blamed Mary for depriving her of the Savior's presence on that indelible day in Bethany (see Luke 10:40).

Today the practice continues. We hear at every hand phrases such as, "My wife just doesn't understand me." "Loosen up; everybody does it." Or, "It wasn't really my fault." The second great commandment is breached routinely by those who say, "He started it," or, "She deserved it." Teens and adults alike jokingly attempt to justify behavioral lapses by saying, "The devil made me do it."

When faced with the consequences of transgression, many of us tend to blame someone else rather than to look to ourselves as the source of the discomfort which always accompanies sin. Instead of getting out of a vicious and senseless circle, we fault our neighbor for our pain and try to pass it on. But to repent, we must leave the circle.

The first step in the repentance process has always been simply to recognize that we have done wrong. If we are so hedged about by pride, rationalization, machismo, or a misdirected sense of self-esteem that we are prevented from ever admitting that we are part of the problem, we are in trouble. We then may not even know of our need to repent. We will have no idea whether the Lord is pleased with us or not. We may become "past feeling" (1 Nephi 17:45). But all men, everywhere, must repent (see 3 Nephi 11:32). To fail to do so is to perish (see Luke 13:3; Helaman 7:28).

To excuse misconduct by blaming others is presumptuous at best, and is fatally flawed with regard to spiritual things; for "we believe that men will be punished for their own sins, and not for Adam's transgression" (Articles of Faith 1:2). This means not only that we will not be punished for what Adam did in the Garden of Eden, but also that we cannot excuse our own behavior by pointing a finger at Adam or at anyone else. The real danger in failing to accept responsibility for our own actions is that, until we do accept it, we may never even enter on the strait and narrow path. Misconduct may be pleasant at first, but it will not be so for long. And it will never lead us to eternal life.

Just as foolish as believing that we can "pass it on" is the idea that the satisfaction of being in the circle can somehow excuse any wrongs committed there. This notion is widely shared and is most often expressed by the phrase, "the end justifies the means." Such a belief, if left undisturbed and unchecked, can also impede the repentance process and cheat us out of exaltation. Those who teach it are almost always attempting to excuse the use of improper or questionable means. Such people seem to be saying, "My purpose was to do good or to be happy; therefore, any little lie, or misrepresentation, or lapse of integrity, or violation of law along the way is justified."

In certain circumstances, some say it is okay to conceal the truth; to dig just a small pit for an adversary; to pursue an advantage of some kind, such as superior knowledge or position. "This is just common practice," or "I'm just looking out for Number One," they say. "All's fair in love and war," or "That's the way the ball bounces," they say. But if the means which prompt people to say these things are wrong, no amount of rationalization or verbal whitewash can ever make them right. Nephi said: "Yea, and there shall be many which shall teach after this manner, false and vain and foolish doctrines, and shall be puffed up in their hearts, and shall seek deep to hide their counsels from the Lord" (2 Nephi 28:9).

Some seek to justify their actions by quoting scripture. They often cite Nephi's killing of Laban as an example of the need to violate a law to accomplish a greater good, so that no "nation should dwindle and perish in unbelief" (1 Nephi 4:13). But they forget that Nephi twice refused to follow the promptings of the Spirit and, in the end, agreed to slay this wicked man only when prodded by the Spirit until he was convinced of the greater good. I believe he was also given the assurance that the penalty for shedding innocent blood had been lifted in that one exceptional case, by Him whose right it is to fix and waive penalties.

The truth is that we are judged by the means we employ as well as by the ends we may hope to obtain. It will do us little good at the last day to respond to the Great Judge, "I know I was not all I could have been, but my heart was in the right place."

In fact, there is danger in focusing merely on ends. To some who did, the Savior said: "Many will say to me in that day: Lord, Lord, have we not prophesied in thy name, and in thy name have cast out devils, and in thy name done many wonderful works? And then will I profess unto them: I never knew you; depart from me, ye that work iniquity." (3 Nephi 14:22–23.)

The War in Heaven was essentially about the means by which the plan of salvation would be implemented. It forever established the principle that even for the greatest of all ends—namely eternal life—the means are critical. It should be obvious to all thinking Latter-day Saints that the wrong means can never attain that objective.

The danger in thinking that the end justifies the means lies in making a judgment we have no right to make. Who are we to say that the Lord will pardon wickedness done to attain a perceived "greater good"? Even if the goal is good, it would be a personal calamity to look beyond the mark and to fail to repent of the wrong we do along the way.

Of course we have the right to strive for happiness. But as we do, we should pause every now and then to look to ourselves. We should remember that "wickedness never was happiness" (Alma 41:10). The sweet peace the gospel brings never comes at all when we justify our misconduct or blame others for our unhappiness.

But there is a way out. We need only think about the pointless, irresponsible childhood game I have mentioned and quietly walk away. Face up, quit, get out, confess, apologize, admit the harm, and just plain walk away from the blaming game.

There are so many important things for us to do in mortality. There is not much time to waste on games. We must obtain essential ordinances. We must enter into and keep sacred covenants. We are to "live by every word which proceedeth forth out of the mouth of God" (D&C 98:11). We must love and serve one another. We are to be proved in all things (see D&C 98:14)—even in little things, like the means to ends. There will be trials. There will likely be other circles we will have to leave. How we respond to all of this will turn out to be the real measure of our salvation.

So, to those, including myself, who from time to time have said, "I am not at fault; I was compelled by circumstances to do what I did," I say: "That may be so. But there is grave danger here. If there is any doubt at all, let us simply repent." For, in the words of Job: "If I justify myself, mine own mouth shall condemn me: if I say, I am perfect, it shall also prove me perverse" (Job 9:20).

And to those who say, "I may have done a little wrong, but my purpose was good and I believe God will justify my behavior," my response is, "Maybe so;

but don't count on it." For, in section 137 of the Doctrine and Covenants, the ninth verse, we read "For I, the Lord, will judge all men *according to their works, according to the desire of their hearts*" (emphasis added).

"So now, though childhood virtues lie
Tarnished
And unused, Desire, which once
Brought all things within your grasp,
Will bring this too—and more—if you
But ask."

CHAPTER EIGHT

My Yoke Is Easy

Not too long ago I visited with a young man I had been trying to encourage. I hoped he would become more active and go on a mission. I asked him why he didn't go to church. At the time he gave me some rather feeble reasons and some general promises that he would mend his ways. Apparently, though, he gave my question more thought; because shortly afterwards I received from him a note telling me what he felt about the Church. I would like to share part of that letter with you. This is what he said: "I have no doubts about the Church, or anything like that. It's just that, from the time you are old enough to walk, they put you in church. They make you go to church." (I suppose the "they" he's talking about are parents or bishops or priesthood leaders or someone like that.)

"I have found in a lot of cases it drives kids away from the Church. If they would start when you are young and make it your responsibility and make you feel that it was your idea and that you would be better for it, that would be one thing. But they don't. They make you feel like a heel for not going; or they say if you miss any Church meetings, you get grounded, or you pay some penalty."

Have any of you ever had anything like that happen in your family?

"Or if you go to church, *they* [again, he's talking about the bishop and all the rest of us] "push talks off on you and everything else. If they would just let you come and enjoy the meeting with each other, it wouldn't be so bad."

I'm sure there isn't anyone who hasn't heard something like that, somewhere, sometime. I never had an adequate opportunity to answer that letter; our paths separated shortly afterwards. But I have reread it several times. Even though that young man may never read this, I would like to answer it, because I think it applies to all of us.

The question, as I understand it, is, Why does The Church of Jesus Christ of Latter-day Saints encourage us, through a kind of moral persuasion that this young man called force, to do things we might not otherwise do?

Why does the Church encourage young people to listen to uplifting music, or to groom their hair? Why does it encourage young women to conform to a dress standard? Why does it encourage home teachers to do their home teaching, and not only to do it, but to report to their priesthood leaders about it? Why, in other words, is the Church constantly encouraging us to do things which we might not otherwise want to do?

Let me tell you a story which I think answers the letter about as well as anything could. Some years ago, a young woman I will call Rose, nineteen years old, moved from southern Utah to the Salt Lake Valley. She left home because she could no longer stand to live with her parents. She didn't like the pressures of the society she was living in. She didn't like the restrictions the Church placed on her conduct. She wanted to get away and to be on her own, to live her own life and do the things she wanted to do. The only place she knew to come to was Salt Lake City. So she did. She moved into one of the wards near the downtown area to escape the rules and pressures which had been put on her.

She got an apartment, but she soon discovered she did not have enough money to go around. She started looking for a job. She was lonely. She couldn't find the work she wanted, and her funds started to dwindle. She lived alone in that kind of environment in Salt Lake for about three weeks. More than I suppose she knows, she was at an eternal crossroads.

Then, one Sunday afternoon, a young lady knocked on the door of the girl's apartment. "Are you a member of the Church?" was the question. "Yes." "Well, I have been asked by our bishop to keep track of new people moving into our ward. Four of us share an apartment. One is moving out. We're looking for someone to share expenses. Would you like to move in with us?"

Out of the clear blue sky came this question, almost as an answer to prayer. It was the solution to Rose's money problem. So our young friend from southern Utah said yes. She would like to share expenses. Lonely, susceptible, she moved in and soon had three friends.

About the first thing that was said to her after she moved into the apartment with these three new roommates was, "We all go to church together. We all go to Mutual together. Come with us." And so she went. About the next thing that was said was: "The bishop has asked us to all meet together on a certain night as a family. One night a month the home teachers are going to come. You need to be available on that night. Is that okay?" And so she participated in family nights and home teaching nights.

Here was a lonely girl. She had lived in Salt Lake three weeks. Nobody had come to see her, and now somebody asked her if one night a month she could be available to have somebody come talk to her . . . some good-looking, young, single member of the elders quorum. Talk about force and coercion!

Think back to the letter that I cited earlier. I suppose that seldom has any greater pressure been put on a girl than this girl had put on her to move in and to associate with the members of the Church in that particular ward. She did it because it was her best option. It really didn't require a lot of thought.

Well, she went to church. Opportunities to participate were offered her, and she turned them all down, every one. She said she wasn't a speaker. She had never taught a class. She didn't know if she had a testimony or not; but she doubted it. She had never borne her testimony in her life. She responded to most questions with silence and a deep blush. She stammered. She was shy.

After she had been in the ward a while the bishopric came to call at her apartment one evening. I happen to know this because I was in that bishopric. "Rose," we said, "our Mutual sports director has just moved out of the ward. There are three more basketball games left before the season's end. If you can't do anything else in the world, will you act as the coach for our team for three weeks?"

Now, if there is one thing this girl did know about, it was basketball. She could play rings around most boys I had ever seen. She was a deadeye with a basketball, and even more than that, she was needed. And so she said okay; she would help out—for three games. She didn't have to pretend with the girls on the team. They liked her because she knew what she was talking about.

The end of the season came. A little period of rest came into Rose's life; and then volleyball season started. She was asked to be the ward sports director. "It will be easy," we said, "just like those three games." She accepted. Now, the next athletic season came and went, and she began to feel at home in the ward, and the young girls started to look to her for an example. You know that's about the most powerful kind of pressure that anyone can put on you. Parents know what I am talking about. Some of the young people do, too. There is nothing worse, as far as being forced to do something is concerned, than having people look at you and knowing that they expect you to do something. You hate to let them down.

The next year an interesting event occurred in this girl's life. There were others, but I would like to mention one of them now specifically. The girl had gone out of her way to arrange with a doctor who lived in the ward to come at a particular time to give physical examinations for all the young ladies in the sports program. That would save them expenses and eliminate the problem of making appointments. She had arranged all this for a Friday evening after work and for the following Saturday morning. However, during regular Mutual meeting on Wednesday, the Mutual president got up and said, "We have just received an urgent call from the stake president. We have a stake farm out in the valley. We have some tomatoes out there that need harvesting. We're afraid of frost. He would like to have every soul that can go to that farm go down there on Friday night and help."

Rose jumped to her feet in defense of her girls and she said, "We have scheduled physicals that night." And the Mutual president said, "I'll leave it up to you, Rosie. Would you be willing to cancel them and bring your girls to the farm?"

Now it's not very often that you get a ready-made excuse to not go to the farm. This girl had one. And there, for the first time, I suppose, in front of her peers and in front of leaders with whom she had worked for a year, she was pushed to the question of whether she wanted to give her allegiance to the priesthood of the Church in an hour of need. Without a lot of hesitation, she said: "Sure, we can reschedule those physicals. We'll go. My girls and I will go."

Some people might say that nothing significant happened the rest of that year in this girl's life. But I think one thing is worthy of mention. She was caught up in the program; she lived the gospel and came to love her girls. As a result of her efforts, the basketball team she coached went to the stake finals. And in a contest as exciting as only a girls' basketball game can be, one of her thirteen-year-old players broke her glasses during that final game. She had thick corrective lenses. She had to wear them when she played. They were knocked off. Somebody stepped on them, and they were broken.

Now, this wasn't a catastrophe. It sometimes happens in intense games. As long as no injury results, people usually take little thought about that kind of event. But Rose knew a lot more about the girls on her team than you and I commonly know about those with whom we work in the Church. She knew, for instance, that the girl with glasses came from a large family, that her father was not active in the Church, and that he only reluctantly allowed her to participate in Church activities. Rose knew that the family didn't have much money. She knew that the unexpected cost of those thick-lensed glasses could seriously disrupt the family's budget and bring recriminations against the Church. She knew that as a result the girl might be prohibited from participating in future Church activities.

The little girl was afraid to go home after the game. She was afraid of her father. So Rose offered to accompany her and to explain to her father just what had happened. No parent could have ever asked more from a child than what this young athletic director said and did. Away from home, living the gospel on her own for the first time, and face-to-face with an antagonistic parent, she stood in the living room of the little house and said; "Don't worry about a thing, Brother. The Mutual has a fund to take care of things that get broken."

Now, the Mutual didn't have any such fund. Anyone who has struggled with an activities budget would surely testify that there is no fund anywhere for broken glasses. But this young girl put into practice, perhaps for the first time, the dozens of gospel lessons she had received on love and charity. Claiming no credit for her own great act of generosity, she cheerfully proffered to the head of the family the money for a dozen days of rent on her own apartment, and said, "This is the fund to pay for broken glasses."

Now, what parent wouldn't give everything he or she possessed to rear that kind of daughter? Who would get the credit? Who really ought to receive the credit for that remarkable act? Who ought to get the credit for the change in the life of this girl? I don't suppose you can single out any particular person. I think everyone in her life who had provided any kind of input and any kind of teaching or any kind of persuasion can share in the credit for that act.

Force? Don't talk to me about force. I thank God for The Church of Jesus Christ of Latter-day Saints and for the influence it has on each of us. I shudder to think what I would be if it were not for the Church.

Let me tell you the rest of the story about this girl for I've been close to her over the years. Two or three years later, she was called on a mission to South America. While she was there, I received an assignment to go to Peru. As I always do when I am out of town, I sought the Church so I could go to sacrament meeting. I found one of the wards in Lima, and I went to the chapel. I walked in about two minutes late and I found an empty chair. Right in front of me was Rose.

She didn't know I was there. I'm afraid I disrupted the meeting just a little bit. I tapped her on the shoulder and said, "Hi, how are you?" She turned around. We had quite a homecoming. She couldn't contain herself. She was so full of love and enthusiasm for the gospel, and so excited about seeing somebody who she felt had something to do with her being there, that she broke down and started to cry. I suppose I did too.

Well, I came home. She came home later. It wasn't more than a year or so after that that my wife and I received an invitation to join Rose to celebrate her temple marriage. I don't know where she would be if it were not for the gospel of Jesus Christ and the influence of her associates in the Church.

I think that we all ought to be more appreciative of the things which the Lord gives us through the Church. The rewards of service in the kingdom are well worth the price. Peace of mind and happiness and joy and love for others result from living the gospel within the framework of The Church of Jesus Christ of Latter-day Saints. There is no other way to find that reward.

To you who complain about people calling you to remind you of meetings, about the priesthood advancement program that seems to want to make you do things that you wouldn't otherwise do, about force and persuasion: Don't ever say that the rewards for involving people in living the gospel aren't worth the effort it takes to achieve that involvement. Where would Rose be if somebody hadn't taken the time to do that for her?

The Savior called the discipline which we sometimes react against in the Church a collar or a yoke. He said, "My yoke is easy, and my burden is light" (Matthew 11:30). I want you to know that I believe that. I testify to you, in all seriousness, that the gospel of Jesus Christ is true, and that it is the means on earth whereby we may perfect ourselves to the point where we can achieve life eternal with our Father in Heaven.

Could I but break the prison of all
I've done before,
And put off the former man,
No fear of welcome would ever slow
My anxious homebound
Step again.

CHAPTER NINE

The Gift of Knowing

Upon graduating from law school, I was fortunate to obtain a position as a clerk at the Utah Supreme Court. I became intimately acquainted with the workings of the court, and came to know personally the judges who presided there. Part of my work was to review and outline the facts of a particular case, to research the applicable law, and then to play the role of what is sometimes called the devil's advocate with the judge who would eventually write the opinion deciding the matter. This was an exciting and challenging time for me. I vividly remember listening to the persuasive arguments of the lawyers for the opposing parties and being swayed first by one and then by the other as case after case was argued on appeal.

Some years later, after leaving the court and becoming a practicing attorney, I had occasion to use the law library at the state capitol. There I happened to meet the chief justice, whom I knew well. He invited me into his office to chat about old times. As we talked about the law and the problems of the practice, our conversation turned to the administrative challenges of running the court. My friend the chief justice was weary. In a few months he would be old enough to retire and leave contention and controversy to others. He indicated that he had given serious thought to doing just that.

"What would *you* think if I retired?" he asked.

Although I could understand the reasons why he might want to escape from the heavy responsibility of the court, I blurted out my instinctive reaction to his question.

"Oh, Judge," I said, "please don't do that. You will never know how comforting it is to those of us who practice here to have someone on the court who always tries to do what's right."

Now, that was not a sophisticated or a reasoned response to his question. It was unlawyerlike on my part, I suppose. But it was a heartfelt and overly simplified statement of truth, intended as a compliment. To my surprise, he became angry. He raised his voice, furrowed his brow, and said, "Heavens, Burt. Any fool can *do* what's right. It's *knowing* what's right that's hard."

He did not mean, of course, that he had a greater ability to do right than anyone else. He did not mean that fools find it easy to obey the law. Nor did he intend to depreciate the difficulty of *doing* anything. My friend had, however, unerringly focused upon his greatest concern as a judge. What he was saying was that, while not everyone applied the law to his own conduct, it was not hard to do so once the law had been determined. It was then a relatively simple matter to do it or not. What was much more difficult was to determine what the law should be, and to decide between two competing, attractive, and well-reasoned alternatives presented by articulate and sophisticated spokesmen. The more difficult thing for him was to choose, to determine, or to decide which of two compelling courses was correct. *That* was hard.

Isn't this true in our lives as well? I do not wish to imply that we are always able to do what we know—to keep the commandments, to pay our tithing, to be honest, and so on (and I know that for most of us these things are hard enough to do). Nevertheless, let me suggest that what is infinitely more difficult is to choose or *know* what to do at the countless crossroads which come into our lives. Especially is this true when the choices presented to us all appear to be equally persuasive or attractive.

Let me illustrate. Imagine with me that you are a college student. It is eight-thirty in the morning. You got up late because you went to bed late. You have an assignment due in your nine o'clock class. You have not finished it. You are not presentable, and you haven't had breakfast. You know that you might possibly make it to class on time if you hurry and remain hungry.

It also occurs to you that, if you stayed home and worked on the assignment all day, you could type it up in finished form. You could then put yesterday's date on it and hand it in tomorrow. You could tell the professor that it was done on time, but that you had a one-hundred-degree fever, or the twenty-four-hour flu, and couldn't get out of bed. Part of that might be true.

What do you do? You know you should tell the truth. You know that you should be in class. You know about integrity. These absolute values are known. If you were asked questions regarding them in the abstract, you would clearly know what the answers should be. However, in the context of the end justifying the means, it might also seem important that you get your assignment in, that you not fail the class, that you keep faith with your parents who are paying your tuition, and that you stay on track in your major subject so as to be able to graduate. And so, what might be simple in isolation becomes a complex problem of daily living for you. It is easy to rationalize and say: "It is too late to get to class now. It would do no good to hurry. Play it cool. Everyone calls in sick once in a while. The professor will never know."

Every day, choices come into our lives which constantly require us to apply what we know. Doing what we know is right is then relatively easy. Knowing what to do in the face of competing, conflicting choices is more difficult.

Let me give you another example. Imagine with me again. You have been looking for a job for months. You are behind on your car payments and, unless you get some money soon, the finance company will repossess your automobile. It is early on a rainy November morning. You are on your way to the most promising job interview you have ever had. Once again, you are late. The gas gauge indicates that you will have just enough fuel to get there, if you are lucky. You slow down for a stoplight and see an acquaintance standing in the rain at the bus stop. You know that if you give your friend a ride, you will be even later for your interview. You know that unless you exceed the speed limit you won't arrive at the appointed hour. You know that if you get another moving violation you will lose your license.

A decision must be made—what do *you do?* If it could be broken down, all of us would know what should be done on any individual item. You should not speed; you should stop for gas; you should give your friend a helping hand; and, of course, the job is important to your financial well-being and happiness. It merits almost any honorable effort to obtain it. But out of all of this, what do *you do?* Either you stop, or you don't. Either you speed, or you do not. Does it matter if you break the law this once? Does it matter if you get the job? Does it matter if you lose your license? Is it important if you fail to give your friend a ride? Are there hidden and unforeseen consequences of possibly running out of gas, or driving too fast? Are there eternal consequences as well?

In such instances, knowing what to do can be most difficult; and the consequences of making wrong choices can be permanent and irretrievable. Going or not going to a class, getting too close to sin, stopping in the wrong place, or failing to stop at all, obeying or disregarding moral laws or the laws of the land—all of these things may eternally affect the course of your existence. What then to do? How do we find the right course? And having found it, how do we stay on it?

It is relatively easy to stay on the strait and narrow path as long as traffic is light and the road is marked. All we have to do is hold the course. But at frequent moments along the way we meet others who are living their lives and exercising their free agency. Without wanting it to be so, we find their demands and expectations influencing our behavior and coloring our choices. Testing times come when friends say, "Come on; don't be a spoilsport," or, "It's okay, everybody does it," or, "No one will know."

At such moments we discover that it is not easy to see, let alone steadily pursue, our course. We find that it is difficult to prepare in advance answers to all of life's questions. We come to know that there are many unmarked junctions in mortality, and that we often arrive at them in the dark, without signposts or road maps to help us select the way.

In other words, the problem of applying what we know to the choices which confront us every day in the world is never easy. The challenges of gospel living come to us not in circumstances of our own choosing, not necessarily one at a time, not often in the classroom, but in situations which we do not fully control.

All of us want the good life; all of us want to be honest and virtuous and to do good to all men. These ultimate values have been pronounced good by God himself. None of us would argue with them, and indeed could not.

But believing in being honest is one thing. It is still another to *be* honest when the forces of daily life make it appear advantageous to be otherwise. Professing concern for others is one thing, but choosing to serve others at an interchange where our own convenience and benefit are prominently present is a real test of our commitment to the second great commandment.

To see our way clearly through the conflicts of everyday living so as to find the course which will ultimately prove to be the best course—that is hard. This is because in much of life the rules have not been revealed, the way is not lighted, and there is no precedent. Each of us must find and walk his or her own path to perfection. While the scriptures provide much help, and we can profit from the experiences of others, the fact remains that life is full of lonely moments in which we alone decide what we will or will not do.

It would surprise me very much if the Lord did not know all of this. I am very certain that He wants it to be this way. He tells us, for example: "It is not meet that I should command in all things; for he that is compelled in all things, the same is a slothful and not a wise servant; wherefore he receiveth no reward. Verily I say, men should be anxiously engaged in a good cause, and do many things of their own free will, and bring to pass much righteousness; for the power is in them, wherein they are agents unto themselves. And inasmuch as men do good they shall in nowise lose their reward." (D&C 58:26–28.)

In other words, it is intended that we have a significant measure of discretion and control over our own lives. In areas where we are not commanded, we are to be agents unto ourselves. This means we are not going to be controlled or commanded from heaven in these areas, whether we want to be or not.

Section 98 of the Doctrine and Covenants tells us why this is so. Simply stated, we are on probation. The Lord says: "And I give unto you a commandment, that ye shall forsake all evil and cleave unto all good, that ye shall live by every word which proceedeth forth out of the mouth of God. For he will give unto the faithful line upon line, precept upon precept; and I will try you and prove you herewith. . . . For I have decreed in my heart, saith the Lord, that I will prove you in all things, whether you will abide in my covenant, even unto death, that you may be found worthy. For if ye will not abide in my covenant ye are not worthy of me." (D&C 98:11–12, 14–15.)

Mortal probation requires that God's children make conscious choices. Were it otherwise, the Lord could not determine who we really are and what we really want. I am speaking here of this area—where no specific counsel or commandments have been given, where it is not known what to do or how to do it, where free agency is in absolute sway. This is the sphere of which my friend on the supreme court said, "It is knowing what's right that's hard."

We must recognize that throughout our lives we will be required to choose between duty, or obligation, and other more or less attractive alternatives. Should we watch television or go visiting teaching? Should we spend time with the family or with friends? Do we read the scriptures or the latest novel? Do we go into debt or do without? Each of these choices, when made, excludes others. Were it otherwise, there could be no real probation. The Designer of the plan of salvation made it that way. By watching and observing where our hearts are, as demonstrated by the free choices we make, He then knows who and what we really are.

Often we are required to choose between two good things. This is one of the paradoxes of modern Christianity. For example: There is a direct relationship between the amount of time spent on a particular calling and the amount of good one can do. A bishop does much good by visiting a needy member. He does ten times as much good by visiting ten needy members. How much time should he spend visiting? Another example: We get close to the Lord by studying the scriptures and pondering them. We get closer still by studying harder and pondering more. How much, then, should we study? A third: A good father spends time with his family. A better father spends more time—and he has a regular weekly evening out with his wife.

Where is the line to be drawn? When is enough, enough, and more, too much? How can we tell if we are active enough, serving others enough, loving enough, home enough? When should we adjust the balance to avoid jeopardizing our salvation?

Aristotle once said: "It is no easy task to be good. For in everything it is no easy task to find the middle. . . . Anyone can get angry—that is easy—or give or spend money; but to do this to the right person, to the right extent, at the right time, with the right motive, and in the right way, *that* is not for everyone, nor is it easy; wherefore goodness is both rare and laudable and noble." (Aristotle, *The Nichomachean Ethics,* trans. David Ross [Oxford: Oxford University Press, 1980], book 2, sec. 9, p. 45.)

Could a man be a better husband if he spent every evening at home with his wife? Could he be a better husband if he had no children, thereby having all of his spare time to dedicate to her? The answer is a resounding no! No one—husband, wife, children, or church—has the claim on the full time of someone else. Children whose parents were with them all of the time would be overshadowed and become dependent. If the Church had full-time bishops, it would have a paid ministry, which could become an end in itself. We have, instead, a divine organization whose ministers are called to help perfect the individual children of God.

It is impossible to provide detailed instructions for each person and circumstance, because the balance varies according to the specific needs and abilities of each individual member of the Church. But somewhere short of total commitment to each of the great causes of family, church, employment, and self there is a balance that is desirable—and not only desirable, but obviously necessary because of time limitations imposed upon us by our Creator. Let us not make the mistake of criticizing the inheritance of time given us by our Father. Let us rather look at what He would have us do with the time we have been given.

There are certain areas of stewardship that we must enter. They are not, and indeed must not be, mutually exclusive. Each requires time. It takes time to be a father, a Relief Society president, a missionary, a student. Service takes time. Inevitably, there are conflicts. But the secret of better performance in one area may not necessarily be to improve in that area at the expense of another. The Lord did not intend that we be at ease in Zion (see 2 Nephi 28:24). He has told us "that all these things are [to be] done in wisdom and order" (Mosiah 4:27).

We must strike a balance. Proper balance usually does not mean that we go down one road as far as we can go, to the exclusion of all other roads. Rather, it is to go down as many roads as necessary, and not more, no further than we must in order not to impede our progress on other paths which our Father also expects us to walk. But which paths should we walk, and how far? When should we begin, and where? And how can we be sure that among the many ways we have chosen well one way, and that the course of our lives is pleasing to the Lord?

It seemed I heard a voice which said,
"O ye
Who must needs change. How oft
I would have gathered thee. The door
Is open wide. The hour is late.
Come home."

CHAPTER TEN

Choices and
More Choices

Thomas Griffith, a contributing editor for *Time* magazine, once summarized the problem this way, reflecting on his choices when he was a young man:

I thought myself happy at the time, my head full of every popular song that came along, the future before me. I could be an artist, a great novelist, an architect, a senator, a singer: having no demonstrable capacity for any of these pursuits made them all appear equally possible for me. All that mattered, I felt, was my inclination; I saw life as a set of free choices. Only later did it occur to me that every road taken was another untaken, every choice a narrowing. A sadder maturity convinces me that, as in a chess game, every move helps commit one to the next, and each person's situation at a given moment is the sum of the moves he has made before. (Thomas Griffith, *The Waisthigh Culture* [New York: Grosset & Dunlap, 1959], p. 17.)

If this is so, then it becomes urgently important, as Elder Richard L. Evans used to say, that we be "where we ought to be, when we ought to be there," and that we be "doing what we should do, when it ought to be done." For we will be judged by the choices we have made, and the balance we have struck becomes what we are.

It is noteworthy that, as Socrates sought the solution to these questions, he asked whether the ability to choose correctly the right road could ever be acquired by man, when he has never been there and doesn't know the way. He determined that the gift of always making wise choices was beyond mortal ability to obtain. It could not be purchased, learned, or acquired by nature. "[It] is shown as coming to us, whenever it comes, by divine dispensation," he said. (See Plato, Meno, in *Great Dialogues of Plato*, trans. W. H. D. Rouse [New York: The New American Library of World Literature, 1956], p. 58.)

Isn't that interesting? A man reputed to be one of the world's wisest, when face-to-face with the question of how to get from where he was to where he knew he should be, threw in the towel. The ability to wisely walk that road, he concluded, had to come by divine dispensation and not by man's own intellect or will.

Now you have the problem. What is the answer? Can we, as Latter-day Saints, expect to fare any better as we make decisions or attempt to find balance in our lives? As a humble servant of the Lord, I testify that we can. Let me tell you why.

At the conclusion of the first day of the Savior's ministry among the Nephites, He taught them to pray: "Ye must always pray unto the Father in my name," He said, "and whatsoever ye shall ask the Father in my name, which is right, believing that ye shall receive, behold it shall be given unto you" (3 Nephi 18:19–20).

I have often thought that this occasion was the greatest teaching moment in the recorded history of the world. The Nephites had only recently experienced the destruction of their cities, the death of loved ones, the separation of families, the loss of homes and worldly possessions. They had survived turmoil and horror. They had known three days of total, impenetrable darkness. Of all the peoples on earth, they had much to pray for.

Then they heard a voice from heaven and saw the Son of Man descend from the sky. They heard him speak to them. Every word that he said must have been permanently engraved upon their hearts. Under these circumstances, Jesus Christ promised them that *whatever they should ask the Father, which was right, would be given unto them.* After He departed from them and ascended into heaven, they remembered that. The scripture records that they dispersed. What they had seen and heard was noised abroad among the people before it was yet dark. Many people labored all the night, that they might bring others to be on the morrow in the place where Jesus should show himself.

And when the morrow came, the Twelve who had been chosen to lead the people caused them to kneel on the face of the earth and pray as they had been taught the day before. Of one mind, they prayed to the Father in the name of Jesus. Remembering His promise, they asked for that which they most desired. And of all the things that they could have prayed for—the restoration of health or of homes, the reuniting of loved ones, the healing of the sick and the wounded, help for their leaders or for their enemies— what was it they asked for? The scripture says simply: "They desired that the Holy Ghost should be given unto them" (3 Nephi 19:9).

The Nephites undoubtedly had in mind the teachings of Nephi himself when he explained the function and purpose of the Holy Ghost. He had asked: "And now, my beloved brethren, after ye have gotten into this strait and narrow path [which is to enter the Church by baptism and to receive a remission of sins and the gift of the Holy Ghost], I would ask if all is done? Behold, I say unto you, Nay. . . . Ye must press forward with a steadfastness in Christ, having a perfect brightness of hope, and a love of God and of all men. Wherefore, if ye shall press forward, feasting upon the word of Christ, and endure to the end, behold, thus saith the Father: Ye shall have eternal life." (2 Nephi 31:19–20.)

And then he added—most significantly, I believe—"For behold, again I say unto you that if ye will enter in by the way, and receive the Holy Ghost, *it will show unto you all things what ye should do*" (2 Nephi 32:5, emphasis added).

Is it any wonder, then, that the Nephites wanted—above everything else—the Holy Ghost? Without Him, without the ability to know all things they should do, they had no hope of returning to their Father; they had no hope of successfully making right choices which would lead them to happiness and eternal life. They knew that the Holy Ghost provides the gift that Socrates sought.

The Nephites, after just one day with the Savior, understood perhaps better than we do the terms of their probation. They comprehended the necessity of divine intervention in their lives so as to assist them in finding their way home.

Much mention is made in the Church of the gift of the Holy Ghost. Each of us who has been baptized has this gift. Collectively, and individually if we are worthy, it sets us apart and makes us different from all other people on the face of the earth. That statement may sound arrogant or presumptuous to some. I intend no offense. But either the gift means something, or it does not. And if it does, we might best discover what it means, lest we find ourselves grouped with the man who had received one talent and who, being afraid to use it, went and hid it in the earth. The Lord scolds him for not taking advantage of such a valuable gift, and He takes it from him. (See Matthew 25:14–30.)

It is difficult for me to illustrate this principle— not because I do not know the Holy Ghost, but because most of my encounters with Him are too personal to recount here. Nevertheless, let me try to show how the Holy Ghost has operated in my life, how He may operate in yours, and how we are unlike other people as a result.

A good number of years ago I found myself on a bus that was loaded with young men from all over the country. We were arriving at Castle Air Force Base in California to attend summer camp. We were cadets aspiring to be commissioned as second lieutenants in the United States Air Force. As the bus entered the field, we got off and were met by a regular Air Force captain, who assembled us in companies on the parade ground. Suitcases, duffel bags, and civilian clothes were everywhere. We were given directions to the barracks and to the commissary. We were told to report in dress uniforms at two o'clock that afternoon on the parade grounds. I was assigned to lead the first company away.

It was an interesting summer. We spent much time in the classroom, some on the firing line, and some in the air. Each week there was a rotation of assignments: we all drew our fair share of disagreeable duty; and each week cadet officers were appointed to participate in special leadership training programs and to direct the lives of the rest of us.

As the summer wore on, I became aware that I had not received a leadership assignment. As camp drew to an end and the last duty rosters were posted, I noticed that I had been overlooked as a cadet commander. Knowing that my success or failure in the Air Force depended in part on how well I performed in this capacity, I asked for and received an appointment to see the officer in charge of the camp.

At the proper hour, I presented myself at his office. I saluted. When the officer asked what I wanted to discuss, I told him that I had noticed a mistake in the duty roster, that I had not been given the rotating assignment of cadet commander. Without even looking up from his desk, the captain told me that he knew that, that he had already decided that I had no future in the Air Force. As I started to protest, he said, "You remember the day that you got off the bus? I asked you to march the men to the barracks. As I watched you, I knew that you did not have what it takes to be an officer in the Air Force. The duty roster stands. You are dismissed."

A flood of thoughts came to my mind. Years of preparation were suddenly of no avail. The course of my life hung in the balance. I turned to leave. There was a silent prayer in my heart—a questioning prayer, really. "Did I come this far to fail?" I asked. I found myself immobilized in front of the captain's desk. I struggled for words. My career was important to me. To my own surprise, I clicked my heels together, saluted smartly, and, without having taken thought of what I should say, I said, "Begging the captain's pardon, sir, but I was under the impression that we were going to be graded by what we learned while we were here, and not by what we knew when we came."

Now, normally that is not the way you talk to regular Air Force officers. There was no precedent for what I did or said. At the time I didn't know from what source came the courage to say those words. But I knew that I was at a crossroads. My future activities and associates would be different, depending on what happened at that moment. My temptations and trials would be different, depending upon what happened at that moment. I would be an enlisted man or an officer, depending on what happened at that moment. The course of my life hung in the balance, as so often happens with seemingly little things.

The captain got up from his desk; he nearly bit his cigar in two. He was obviously unaccustomed to that kind of insubordination. He walked around to where I stood. He looked at my shoes; he looked at my uniform; he looked at my double chin, as I held myself at strict military attention. For at least five minutes, although it seemed much longer, he circled me, time after time. I stood there, not knowing what else to do. Finally he said, "I might have been wrong about you. Maybe you do have what it takes to be an officer in this man's Air Force. We'll change the duty roster;

you can command your company during the last week's activities. We'll see what you can do."

Do I believe that the Holy Ghost prompted me in what I said and did that day? Yes, I do. Could not someone else, a non-Latter-day Saint perhaps, have said the same thing, or something better, so as to achieve the same result? I don't know. What I do know is that for me, in that moment, in that place, what I said and did was right. Someone else may have been more articulate. Someone else may not have gotten into the difficulty in the first place. Someone else may have turned on his heel and left upon being informed of the captain's displeasure. The course of that person's life would have been different than mine.

I have never looked back on that incident. I am certain that what happened was right. I have no regrets, nor have I ever given more than passing thought to what might have become of me had I left the office and the Air Force at that moment.

I know that one of our greatest blessings as Latter-day Saints is that we need never look back. We need never ask what might have been. Should I have dropped out of school or should I have struggled to get my degree? Should I have married Sally instead of the girl I did marry? What if I had gone on a mission or married in the temple?

If we have been worthy, and if we have followed the guidance of the Spirit as manifested in the feelings of our hearts, then we can know beyond doubt that what is done is best. Although we may have weathered trials, although we may be having difficulties, we can be certain that we are where the Lord would have us be. Although the grass may seem greener elsewhere, we can know that our decision to enter the pasture we are in was prompted and purposeful and preparatory.

Knowing these things, and knowing that we have done—for the most part—what the Lord wanted done, can bring peace and joy beyond expression. No other people on earth can ever have *this* blessing, for it comes from having the companionship of the Holy Ghost.

As I have better understood my relationship with the Holy Ghost, I have come to know what it is to

- Unexpectedly change airplanes in a distant city . . . only to find after arriving home that the first scheduled flight had been indefinitely delayed.
- Begin interviewing a missionary with the question, never asked before or since, "Elder, who have you been fighting with?" . . . and to hear the astonished reply, "President, how did you know?"
- Pay a surprise visit to a distant city . . . only to hear someone say, "I have been praying for days that you would come."

Occasionally I have had time to pray and ponder before acting on the promptings of the Comforter. More often, I have found myself, as Nephi was, "led by the Spirit, not knowing beforehand the things which I should do" (1 Nephi 4:6).

The Lord told Joseph and Oliver, "It shall be given thee in the very moment what thou shalt speak and write" (D&C 24:6).

To Thomas B. Marsh, He said, "Go your way whithersoever I will, and it shall be given you by the Comforter what you shall do and whither you shall go" (D&C 31:11).

What to say! What to write! Where to go! What to do! Such guidance, if given infrequently for only some of life's decisions, would be priceless. But the broader promise was given to the Prophet Joseph at Salem, Massachusetts, that "the place where it is my will that you should tarry, for the main [or for the most part] shall be signalized unto you by the peace and power of my Spirit, that shall flow unto you" (D&C 111:8). He—in company with Oliver Cowdery and David Whitmer—was also told that the Holy Ghost would manifest "all things which are expedient unto the children of men" (D&C 18:18).

This is of monumental significance. It makes it easier to understand why President Marion G. Romney said in the April general conference of 1974, "The importance of receiving the gift of the Holy Ghost is beyond expression" (*Ensign*, May 1974, p. 92). But, "beyond expression" must not mean beyond reverent thankfulness or beyond understanding. The world may not comprehend that the Holy Ghost manifests the "truth of all things" (Moroni 10:5). We know that He does.

The Lord told the Prophet Joseph Smith, "God shall give unto you knowledge by his Holy Spirit, yea, by the unspeakable gift of the Holy Ghost, that has not been revealed since the world was until now; which our forefathers have awaited with anxious expectation to be revealed in the last times, which their minds were pointed to by the angels, as held in reserve for the fulness of their glory" (D&C 121:26–27).

The gift has been given. What we make of it is up to us. Unless we listen to counsel, we will receive none. Unless we pray, exercise faith, love, obey, and keep the tabernacles of our spirits clean, we can have no claim upon this unspeakable gift.

I will. I will. Could there be place
For me?
There is. A place to grow and serve
And somehow be a part. To sing
A song of redeeming love. Be still,
My joyful heart.

CHAPTER ELEVEN

Being Realistic About Television

"When I was a child, I spake as a child, I understood as a child, I thought as a child: but when I became a man, I put away childish things" (1 Corinthians 13:11).

One of the most important things standing in the way of our changing for the better is the fixation that many of us have with television and other electronic wizardry. Computers, video players, and electronic games are an inescapable part of modern life. They represent much that is progressive and good in the world. But they have a dark side as well.

Just for a moment, I would like to speak to you as if you were a child. My hope is that my words will not be condescending, but that even the smallest child can understand them.

Let me talk about your home. Let me ask you: Who is most important there? How do you decide who is most important? Is it the person who earns the most? Is it the person you love the most? Is it the one who gives you the most of his or her time? Is it the person who has the best room? Who, truly, is most important in your home? You might answer that no one is more important than anyone else in your family. I wonder if that is really true.

Let me ask the question another way: How is the TV treated in your home? Does it have its own room? Do you like it better than your brother? Your mother? Do you like it better than your great-grandfather? Does it get much rest? Do your parents spend more time with it than they do with you? Do they spend more money on it than they do on you?

Do you value the TV's opinions more than those of your parents? Does it tell you what to eat for breakfast? Does it come to dinner? Often? When it does, does it get the best seat? Do you have to keep quiet when it is talking? Does it ever cause fights in your house? Have you ever been sent to your room when it did?

Who really is the boss in your family? Is it the TV? Does it tell you what to do? Does it tell you when to go to bed? What about on Saturday? Does it tell you what to do then? Does it tell you when to go to a friend's house? Does it talk during prayers? Does it tell the home teachers when it is time to go? Does it ever keep you from going to church? What about on Super Bowl Sunday?

Is the TV your best friend? Would you be lonely without it? Would you cry if it broke? Would you miss it more than you might miss your sister? If your house were on fire and you could only save one thing, would you save the television? What if you could save two things? Could you live without TV for a week? How about a month?

Who is your favorite teacher? Is it the TV? Do you like TV better than Sunday School? How about seminary? Does TV teach the same things as your seminary teacher does? Does it teach different things? Who is right?

Does TV make you want things you don't have? Does this make you happy? Does it ever make you angry at your parents? What about when they won't buy you something you have seen advertised on TV?

Whom do you want to be like when you grow up? A TV star? Do you want to live like the rich and famous? Is your dad as cool as Cosby? Is your mom too much like Roseanne? Is your wardrobe out of date? Who told you so? Was it the TV? Does TV always tell the truth?

Somebody once said that TV was chewing gum for the eyes. Think about it.

Jesus said, in the Sermon on the Mount: "Lay up for yourselves treasures in heaven, . . . for where your treasure is, there will your heart be also" (Matthew 6:20–21). This means that the things to which you give your time, attention, and money are the things that are really important to you. Unless these things are also important to the Lord, they aren't going to count for much in heaven.

Someone once said, "The real trouble with TV is not so much the trouble it causes but the behavior it prevents." Some other quotes I like are these:

"It [TV] leads not to human interaction, but rather toward withdrawal into private communication with the picture tube and the private life of fantasy. It is aimed less often at solving the problems of life than escaping from them. It is essentially a passive behavior—something a child surrenders himself to, something that is done to and for him, something that he doesn't have to work for or think about or pay for." (Wilbur Schramm, quoted in Nicholas Johnson, *Test Pattern for Living* [New York: Bantam Books, 1972], p. 46.)

And how about this one: "There is such a thing as psychological suicide in which one does not take his own life by a given act, but dies because he has chosen—perhaps without being entirely aware of it—not to live" (Rollo May, quoted in *Test Pattern for Living*, p. 50).

Does watching TV or playing electronic games prevent you from really living, from doing things that you should do? Does it keep you from being a friend, or going to seminary, or helping with the dishes, or doing work for your great-grandfather? If it does, do you think it is really your friend? Maybe it is not your best friend. Maybe the Savior would want you to find better company, at least some of the time.

Long before television, there was a great playwright named Henrik Ibsen. He wrote a play called *Peer Gynt*. It is a story about a young man in Scandinavia who lived his life by doing whatever he wanted to. He grows old during the course of the play. Near the end, he is chased by a button molder who wants to melt his body down, to recycle it for something more worthwhile—buttons.

Peer runs across the frozen ground trying to escape from this man. As he does, some tumbleweeds get under his feet. He yells at them and says, "Get out of my way. Off with you. You block my path." And then something very interesting happens. The weeds speak back to him and say: "We are thoughts.

You should have thought us. Feet to run on you should have given us. . . . We should have soared up like clangorous voices, and here we must roll along as weeds."

He kicks them out of his way and keeps on running. After a while he steps on some leaves. The leaves begin to talk too, and say: "We are watchwords. You should have proclaimed us. Your dozing has riddled us. Worms have gnawed us in every crevice, and we have never been able to bear fruit."

The wind blows in his face and whispers to him: "We are songs. You should have sung us. A thousand times over you have cowed us down and smothered us. Down in the heart's pit we have laid and waited, but we were never called forth."

Peer becomes angry as a result of these accusations. "Poison you," he says. "Have I time for verse and stuff? I am running for my life." Then he bumps into a tree. There are dewdrops dripping from its branches. They speak to him as well. "We are tears unshed forever. Ice spears sharp and wounding. We could have melted. Now our barb is in the bosom. The wound is closed over and our power to help is gone."

Peer doesn't like that too much either, but he still keeps on running. Finally he trips over some straws and falls on his face. As he struggles to get up, the straws reproach him, too. "We are deeds. You should have achieved us. Doubt, the throttler, has crippled and torn us. On the Day of Judgment, we'll come aflock and tell the story; then woe to you."

"We are thoughts. You should have thought us." . . . "We are words. You should have proclaimed us." . . . "We are songs. You should have sung us." . . . "We are tears. You should have shed us." . . . "We are deeds. You should have achieved us." . . . "And on the Judgment day, woe to you." (See Henrik Ibsen, *Peer Gynt* 5. 6.)

One of the great cries of this generation is that it doesn't have time to do the things it should do. We don't work on our family history because we don't have time. We don't love our neighbors because we don't have time. And yet we spend more time watching television than on doing any other single elective thing. I don't believe the excuse will hold up on Judgment Day. We will never be able to claim that we didn't have time. All we can possibly say in our own defense is that our priorities were not the same as the Lord's.

It is imperative for us to "lay aside childish things." As we live out our lives, we should magnify the things we know; seek to know more; and order our priorities so as to lay up treasures in heaven. As we do, there will be time for all of the important things—even for responsible and prudent television watching.

"And he arose, and came to his father.
But when he was yet a great way off,
His father saw him, and had compassion,
And ran, and fell on his neck,
And kissed him."

CHAPTER TWELVE

Never Stop Trying

In the following paragraphs I adapt a fascinating story I once read about a small village on a dry and desolate coast in South America.

One day the inhabitants of this village were visited by a remarkable person. He was tall; they were short. He was fair; they were dark-skinned. He came from beyond the sea and was shrouded with mystery. They were plain, illiterate, and isolated. They thought he was the most handsome man in the world. They called him Esteban, which in their language meant "crown" or "king."

They believed that this stranger, by the power of his word, could cause fish to jump out of the sea. He could bring forth springs of water from the rocky cliffs by merely commanding the water to flow.

They were concerned about his size, for he seemed condemned to go through their doorways sidewards; he was always cracking his head on the ceiling beams of their small adobe houses. He often stood, in order to avoid the embarrassment of not fitting into their furniture, perhaps even breaking it. But they loved him just the same.

When at last it came time for him to leave, they fought for the privilege of carrying him on their shoulders. They strewed flowers in his path and invited him to come back if he wished, whenever he wished.

After he had gone they did not need to look at one another to see that *they* were no longer the same, and that they would never be the same again. Because they had known Esteban, they knew that everything would be different from then on. Then they proceeded to do an incredible thing. They built wider doors, higher ceilings, and stronger furniture in their houses. They prepared their homes so that Esteban, when he returned, could go anywhere he wanted and feel at ease.

They also painted their house fronts in bright colors to help make his memory eternal. Because they had seen him bring forth water from the rocky cliffs, they nearly broke their backs digging for water there also. When they found it, they planted flowers among the stones in his honor.

It was said that, years later, as ships first sailed around the Horn, passengers would be almost suffocated by the smell of flowers on the high seas. Ships' captains would come down from their bridges and point to a promontory of roses on the horizon. "Look there," they would say, "where the wind is so peaceful, over there where the sun is so bright that the sunflowers don't know which way to turn; there where white-walled homes are hidden by trees. Yes, over there. That is Esteban's village. There where the color of flowers is splashed over the hillside, there are Esteban's people." (Adapted from Gabriel Garcia Marquez, "The Handsomest Drowned Man in the World," in *Leaf Storm and Other Stories*, trans. Gregory Rabassa [New York: Avon Books, 1972], pp. 145–54.)

While that particular story is fictional, there are some threads of truth in it. There are countless similar legends told in Latin America. All of them have their origin in the visit of the Savior to the Western Hemisphere. But isn't it interesting to contemplate that a man could be so loved that his visit could change the lives of the people he visited?

Could this not be, in part, what it means to take upon ourselves the name of Christ? His followers are clearly expected to change their lives. There is evidence of this in the Book of Mormon. In the last days of King Benjamin's reign, that great prophet called his people together and gave them a stirring address concerning the conditions under which they might gain salvation. The effect of the king's words was so powerful that, after hearing him, the people reported that they were willing to change their lives, to enter into a covenant with God to do His will all the remainder of their days. Upon receiving this response, Benjamin said: "Ye have spoken the words that I desired; and the covenant which ye have made is a righteous covenant. And now, because of the covenant which ye have made ye shall be called the children of Christ, his sons, and his daughters; for behold, this day he hath spiritually begotten you; for ye say that your hearts are changed through faith on his name." (Mosiah 5:6–7.)

This concept of a changed heart and taking upon ourselves the name of Christ was further taught by Alma the Younger. The scripture tells us that he began to deliver the word of God to the people, first in Zarahemla and then throughout the land. As he counseled his people, he recalled that his father, Alma, had believed the words of Abinadi and had been converted. "According to his faith there was a mighty change wrought in his heart" (Alma 5:12).

Then he reminded his listeners that his father had preached to their fathers and that "a mighty change was also wrought in their hearts" (Alma 5:13). Then he asked this profound question, which can be asked of all of us: "And now behold, I ask of you, my brethren of the church, have *ye* spiritually been born of God? Have *ye* received his image in *your* countenances? Have *ye* experienced this mighty change in *your* hearts?" (Alma 5:14, emphasis added.)

It is clear to me that membership in The Church of Jesus Christ of Latter-day Saints requires a change in the lives of those who profess to follow Christ. We are members of His Church. We know more about Him and when He will come again than any other people who have ever lived. Not only is it possible for us to have a change of heart and to receive His image in our countenances as a result of following His teachings but it is also *expected* that this will happen. It is not possible to be a believing member of the Church without experiencing a transformation, a metamorphosis, or change of form. This change may be imperceptible at first. It may be so subtle that we are unaware that we are changing; but we are. Such a change comes in the lives of those who honor the covenant by being baptized and faithfully remembering Christ.

But it also takes faith to change. Have we done anything to broaden the spiritual beams of our houses and change the environment in which we live in anticipation of the fact that He will soon come again? The Savior told the Prophet Joseph Smith and the elders of the Church: "Prepare yourselves for the great day of the Lord. Watch, therefore, for ye know neither the day nor the hour." (D&C 133:10–11.)

Are we watching and are we waiting? Do we have any personal preparations to finish? Does the parable of the foolish virgins have any significance for us today? When He comes for us will it be too late to do the things we had intended to do to get ready for His coming?

Jacob tells us: "The people of the Lord are they who wait for him" (2 Nephi 6:13). Are we His people?

I would like to propose a five-point test. Anyone can easily use it to help determine whether the change has been deep enough, if the ceiling beams of our hearts are high enough to confidently anticipate the second coming of the Lord Jesus Christ. There is no particular order of importance to these questions. But if you will honestly answer them they will provide a fair analysis of whether you are spiritually prepared for that great event.

Question: Do you get a spiritual thrill or do your eyes mist over when you sing, "Come, O Thou King of Kings" or "Redeemer of Israel?" If not, then perhaps you really don't have the relationship you could have with our Savior.

I recall being in a meeting once with President Spencer W. Kimball. We sang four verses of "Redeemer of Israel." Most of us closed our books and awaited the business of the meeting, when the prophet said: "I have always been most impressed with the fifth verse of that hymn. I wonder if we might not sing it." We reopened our books and looked in the fine print at the bottom of the page, and shared these words, which now bring tears to my eyes every time I hear them. We sang:

> Restore, my dear Savior, the light of thy face;
> Thy soul-cheering comfort impart;
> And let the sweet longing for thy holy place
> Bring hope to my desolate heart.
>
> (*Hymns*, 1985, no. 6.)

Question: When you take the sacrament, do you plan how you intend to remember Him?

When we partake of the sacrament, we specifically covenant to remember Christ. Sometimes we are busy worrying about other things. We center our attention on a noisy child behind us, or on a cute boy or girl at the end of the row. But we could use the worship time in sacrament meeting to plan how we intend to always remember Him. If we don't do this, I think we may have some changes yet to make in our house. Do entire sacrament meetings go by without our thinking of the Savior? If so, then we are a long way from always remembering Him.

Question: Do you really try to keep His commandments? Now, I know that no one of us can perfectly keep them; but do you try?

Sometimes people come to me because I am a General Authority. They want to unburden themselves of things they have done which are inconsistent with the commandments Christ has given. I tell them that what they have done matters less than what they are going to do about it. What matters more is what direction they are going and how serious they are about changing their lives. I believe that once we become so set in our ways that we no longer try to change and bring our lives into conformity with what the Savior would have us be, there is grave danger that we will not be ready when He comes.

Question: Every time a significant decision (or an insignificant one, for that matter) comes up in your life, do you ask yourself, "What would Christ do? What would He have me do?" Then do you do it?

If you do, then your ceiling may be tall enough. If you don't, you may have some remodeling to do.

Question: Do you genuinely want to be associated with Him and to do His work?

If you do, then you will be one of the first to greet Him when He comes. But if you find yourself rationalizing about Church standards or programs, or if you spend your time criticizing the Brethren, or if you have reservations about His gospel, then you are "kicking against the pricks." You have a great repair job to do on that house of yours before you can welcome Him again. The Lord has said, "They shall not be ashamed that wait for me" (2 Nephi 6:7).

Once again quoting Alma the Younger:

> Do you look forward with an eye of faith, . . . to stand before God to be judged according to the deeds which have been done in the mortal body? . . .
>
> Can you imagine to yourselves that ye hear the voice of the Lord, saying unto you, in that day: Come unto me ye blessed, for behold, your works have been the works of righteousness upon the face of the earth? . . .
>
> Can ye look up to God at that day with a pure heart and clean hands? . . . Can you look up, having the image of God engraven upon your countenances? . . .

Behold, I say unto you, . . . if ye have experienced a change of heart, and if ye have felt to sing the song of redeeming love, I would ask, can ye feel so now? . . .

If . . . not ye are not prepared to meet God. Behold ye must prepare quickly; for the kingdom of heaven is soon at hand, and such an one hath not eternal life. (Alma 5:15, 16, 19, 26, 28.)

It seems clear that the Lord expects us to be an ensign to the nations, the salt of the earth, and a light which will so shine that others may see our good works and thereby glorify our Father which is in heaven. If we can come to the relationship with the gospel that we should have, the rest of the world will say, "Look over there. Look at those people. Look at the peace and the beauty which surrounds them. Surely they are the people of the Lord."

Our lives are the greatest testimonies we will ever bear of the fact that we believe and love the Lord. Let us resolve to be numbered among His people, those who constructively wait for His coming.

Index

— A —

Agency, 9, 79
    counterpart to repentance, 36
    example in young woman's
      life, 66–73
Answers, prepared in advance, 80
Appreciation, for the Church, 73
Aristotle, on goodness, 83
Atonement, allows for repen-
    tance, 36
Attitude, defines the character, 50
    of back-row members, 50,
      54–55
Attributes, undesirable, 12

— B —

Back-row members, reluctant to
    pray, 49–50
Balance, 86
    drawing the line, 83
    on the roads of life, 84
    varies with need and ability, 83
Baptism, provides initial cleans-
    ing, 31

covenants, 104
Basketball, used to activate, 69
Blame, put on others, 62

— C —

Cain, blamed God, 58
Challenges, of gospel living, 80
Change, result of repentance, 36
Choices, between two good
    things, 82
    made with integrity, 78
    of duty, 82
    require application of knowl-
      edge, 78
    required in mortal probation,
      82
Church callings, metaphorical
    mountains, 9
Church meetings, 66
Cleansing, result of repentance,
    36
Coffee cans, disposing of, 13–14
Commandments, 106
Consequences, associated with
    choice, 8

can be permanent, 79
unwillingness to accept, 57–58
Countenance, in the image of
Jesus Christ, 104
Covenants, honoring, 104
important in mortality, 62
Criticism, of the Brethren, 107

— D —

Death, a metaphorical mountain,
9
Decisions, 107
Desire, part of repenting, 15
Discipline, required to change, 18
Discomfort, always accompanies
sin, 59
Discouragement, metaphorical
mountain, 9
Doubt, eliminated by repentance
and prayer, 41
Drug abuse, imperils salvation,
14
Duty, 82

— E —

Effort, essential for change,
35–36
necessary for repentance, 7
Electronic games, can preclude
real life, 98
Elite, may blame others for failure, 58
Eternal life, greatest of all "ends,"
61

received through righteousness, 53

— F —

Failure, blamed on others, 58
Faith, dependent on chosen
route, 8
essential for change, 105
fills the glass of life, 30
in Jesus Christ, 27, 103–4
justifies claim upon the Holy
Ghost, 94
must be earned, 7
Faithfulness, to the Church, 55
"Force," 66, 72
Forgiveness, a miraculous gift, 36
reward for repenting, 31
Franklin, Benjamin, listed desirable virtues, 24–25
Friends, help us change, 16
Front-row members, compared to
back-row members, 46–56
Fun, 51
sought before a mission, 52

— G —

Game, "pass it on," 57
Goblets, example of our lives,
29–31
God, hears prayers of parents, 38
Godly sorrow, part of repentance
process, 33–34
Gospel, most important cause, 48
Guilt, shifting the burden of, 58

— H —

Habits, bad, 12
Happiness, from living the
    gospel, 73
    haphazard pursuit of, 30
    striving for, 62
Hazardous waste, like a bad
    habit, 12
Health, dependent on chosen
    route, 8
Hearts, changed through faith in
    Christ, 103–4
    new, 20
Heroes, help change habits,
    23–28
    See also Models
Holy Ghost, can operate in our
    lives, 89–92
    can prompt in all choices,
    93–94
    desired by the Nephites, 88
    manifests all things, 92
    sets us apart from others, 89
    shows us what to do, 88
Home teachers, assigned to non-
    member, 13
Honesty, 80
Honey, in coffee cans, 13–14

— I —

Immorality, imperils salvation, 14
Inactive members, returning to
    activity, 38–41
Instruction, put to the test, 9

Integrity, in making choices, 78

— J —

Jesus Christ, answers questions
    through scriptures, 51–53
    can change lives, 103
    drawing near to, 49
    gave His life, 49
    imaginary conversation with,
    50–53
    on prayer, 87
    remembers sins no more, 35,
    36, 43–44
    taking His name upon us, 104
    visiting the Nephites, 87–89
    will lead us along, 53
    work and glory of, 53
Journals, records of progress, 16
Joy, felt in doing God's will, 93
    from living the gospel, 73
Judgment, according to means em-
    ployed and ends sought, 61
Judgment Day, facing God with
    one's accomplishments, 21

— K —

Knowledge, essential to making
    choices, 78

— L —

Laman and Lemuel, blamed
    Nephi, 58
Latter-Day Saints, to be an en-
    sign to the nations, 108

Leaders, not called from the back
row, 50
Life, dependent on chosen route, 8
has moments of decision, 81
one's greatest testimony, 108
Love, important in mortality, 62
justifies claim upon the Holy
Ghost, 94
results from living the gospel,
73
Loyalty, to the Church, 55

— M —

Marriage, a metaphorical mountain, 9
Members, anxiously engaged,
willing, and reluctant,
45–46
Millennium, back-row crowd will
pay attention to, 49
Missions, metaphorical mountains, 9
of most worth, 52
Models, help us change, 27
not perfect, 27–28
see also Heroes
Mortal probation, requires
choices, 82
Mountains, examples of life, 2

— O —

Obedience, back-row members
show reluctance in, 49
justifies claim upon the Holy
Ghost, 94

Ordinances, important in mortality, 62

— P —

Peace, felt in doing God's will, 93
fills up the glass of life, 30
from living the gospel, 73
looked for within us, 30
received through righteousness, 53
reward for repenting, 31
sweet in the gospel, 62
Pilate, blamed the Jews, 58
Plan of salvation, 61
Prayer, back-row members show
reluctance in, 49
clears doubts, 41
essential for change, 35
justifies claim upon the Holy
Ghost, 94
Preparation, for the Second
Coming, 105–8
Pride, of former believers, 37
prevents recognition of sin, 59
Procrastination, can imperil salvation, 14
Prophet, drawing near to, 49
Prophets, call people to repentance, 37
Prosperity, a metaphorical moun-
tain, 9
Purification, thrilling process, 31

— R —

Rationalization, by quoting scrip-

ture, 60–61
excludes repentance, 55
of Church standards, 107
of the "means," 60
prevents recognition of sin, 59
Recognition, part of repentance
process, 33
Referee, example of a model,
25–27
Remorse, godly sorrow, 33–34
part of repentance process, 33
Renewal, result of repentance, 36
Repentance, a principle of purification, 31
born of the Spirit, 36
clears doubts, 41
counterpart to agency, 36
demands works, 35
disposing of sins, 21
experiences must be earned, 7
learned along the way, 8
like a mountain, 2
must be experienced, 7
necessary for salvation, 10
Restitution, part of repentance
process, 33
Rewards, of service, 73
Roads, courses in life, 84
Romney, Marion G., on receiving
the Holy Ghost, 94

— S —

Sacrament, planning how to remember Christ, 106
Salvation, depends on repentance, 10

imperiled by bad habits, 14
Saul, anointed to be king, 18–20
Scriptures, should be studied
daily, 16–17
Second Coming, test on preparation for, 105–8
Selfishness, helps fill unclean
glass of life, 30
Service, back-row members show
reluctance in, 49
fills the glass of life, 30
important in mortality, 62
in the kingdom 73
takes time, 84
transforming power in, 16
Sickness, a metaphorical mountain, 9
Sin, brings rationalization, 55
difficult to dispose of, 14
does not lead to eternal life, 60
never will be happiness, 30
not overcome by priesthood
blessings alone, 14–15
of former believers, 37
spiritual death, 55
Slothfulness, helps fill unclean
glass of life, 30
Smith, Joseph, on seeing First Vision, 7–8
Socrates, on choosing correctly,
86
Speakers, listened to by members,
45
Spirit, followed with confidence,
92
whispers to the mind, 56

See also Holy Ghost
Stewardships, not mutually exclusive, 84
Strait and narrow path, 79

— T —

Talents, not to be buried, 51
Television, being realistic about, 95–100
  can preclude real life, 98
  poor excuse on Judgment Day, 100
  selection of programs, 16
Temptations, not overcome by priesthood blessings alone, 14–15
  of the easy way, 10
  on spiritual mountains, 9–10
  running way from, 16
Testimony, evident in our lives, 108
  must be earned, 7
Theories, put to the test, 9
Thoughts, clean or unclean, 30

Time, essential to change, 35
  essential to replacement of habits, 18
  inheritance from our Father, 84
  necessary for repentance, 7
  not to be idled away, 51
  spent watching television, 100
Tithing, 51, 55
Trials, important in mortality, 62
  on spiritual mountains, 9–10
Trust, in others, 23
  in the Lord, 27

— W —

War in Heaven, over implementation of plan of salvation, 61
Wickedness, never was happiness, 62
Wisdom, fills the glass of life, 30
Word of Wisdom, 55
Works, part of repentance, 35
Worldly things, laid aside for better, 51